PHILOSOPHY AND REVELATION

This encyclical, dealing with faith and reason and their specific universality, may turn out to be the most important document of the modern Church on the subject of faith and reason and on philosophy understood as a mirror or people's cultures.

Philosophy and Revelation presents an accessible, critical commentary on the *Fides et Ratio* encyclical and the topical faith and reason debate, whilst questioning more deeply the nexus between philosophy and Revelation. The historical introduction of the relation between philosophy and theology through the middle ages, early modern period, and the 19th century to the present, forms an invaluable background to understanding the faith/reason debate and the spirit of the Encyclical. With a focus on truth, reason, metaphysics and wisdom, the author explores philosophy per se and its relationship to a faith reaching for its self-understanding. *Philosophy and Revelation* was first published by Città Nuova in 1999 in Italian under the title *Filosofia e Rivelazione*. This English translation has been completed by Emanuel L. Paparella, University of Central Florida, USA.

D1823462

Ashgate Translations in Philosophy, Theology and Religion

This new series presents the first English language translations of important contemporary and classic works in philosophy, theology and world religions.

Other titles in the series

The Natural Order and Other texts
Asger Jorn translated by Peter Shield

Environmental Ethics and Policy-Making
Mikael Stenmark

Philosophy and Revelation

A contribution to the debate on reason and faith

VITTORIO POSSENTI
University of Venice

Translated by Emanuel L. Paparella
University of Central Florida
from *Filosofia e Rivelazione. Un contributo al dibattito su ragione e fede*
(Città Nuova, Roma, 1999)

Ashgate

Aldershot • Burlington USA • Singapore • Sydney

Published by
Ashgate Publishing Limited
Gower House
Croft Road
Aldershot
Hants GU11 3HR
England

Ashgate Publishing Company
131 Main Street
Burlington, VT 05401-5600 USA

Ashgate website: http://www.ashgate.com

British Library Cataloguing in Publication Data
Possenti, Vittorio
   Philosophy and revelation : a contribution to the debate on
   reason and faith. - (Ashgate translations in philosophy,
   theology and religion)
   1. Religion - Philosophy
   I. Title
   210

Library of Congress Cataloging-in-Publication Data
Possenti, Vittorio.
   [Filosofia e rivelazione. English]
   Philosophy and revelation : a contribution to the debate on reason and faith / Vittorio
Possenti ; translated by Emanuel L. Paparella.
       p. cm. -- (Ashgate translations in philosophy, theology and religion)
   Includes index.
   ISBN 0-7546-1675-4 -- ISBN 0-7546-1676-2 (pbk.)
    1. Philosophical theology. 2. Faith and reason--Christianity. 3. Catholic Church. Pope
(1978- : John Paul II). Fides et ratio. I. Title. II. Series.

   BT50 .P6813 2001
   231'.042--dc21

                                                              2001022057

ISBN 0 7546 1675 4 (Hbk)
ISBN 0 7546 1676 2 (Pbk)

Typeset by Manton Typesetters, Louth, Lincolnshire, UK and printed and bound in Great Britain by MPG Books Ltd, Bodmin, Cornwall.

Contents

Introduction

Besides the catholicity or universality of Revelation issuing from a transcendence to which faith tends, there is also a 'catholicity' or a natural
universality of reason; a reason which is open, flexible, magnanimous,
compassionate, friendly towards everything there is and especially towards
the other's face. This kind of reason can be helpful to postmodern culture in
overcoming its insecurity, the temptation to be satisfied with little and the
consequent risk of going adrift in an enigmatic and uncertain era.

The encyclical *Fides et Ratio*, dealing with faith and reason and their
specific catholicity, may well turn out to be the most important document of
the modern Church on the subject announced in its title and on philosophy
understood as a mirror of peoples' cultures. Its central theme can be identified as the establishment of the right relationship between revealed truth and
truth reached by philosophical knowledge. What follows here can be loosely
situated within the space occupied by the encyclical, although some of its
topics will remain in the background. Since the essay was born as thinking
caused by and reacting to the encyclical, it refrains from making an exegesis
of the document. Our intention rather is that of questioning and reflecting
on the nexus between philosophy and Revelation without excluding a priori
the insights of the same encyclical.[1]

Fides et Ratio seeks to put into motion again faith that thinks (a different
thing from the believer that thinks) and the issue of truth, thus opening up a
higher dialogue with late modernity and postmodernity 'before the silver
thread gets loose, the golden lamp shatters, and the bucket breaks at the
fountain' (*Qo* 12: 6). Among the various stimuli proposed by the encyclical
to revive this belief that thinks, a significant one is the methodology of
collaboration and circularity between reason and faith, philosophy and theology, to their mutual advantage. We would like to pursue the same journey
avoiding negativism, looking rather for the positive and the true, so that the
philosophical *eros* which is potentially present in every man may come alive
through a search that is both ontosophic and contemplative. By contemplative search we mean here a spirit open to and predisposed to keeping the
light of the intellect focused on the whole of reality. By ontosophic search
we mean a search which aims at attaining a wisdom of being capable of
disclosing its original native flavour.

The focus of our brief treatment can be identified in a few key words:
philosophy, Revelation, truth, faith, reason, metaphysics, wisdom; words
which in their plurality may point to heterogeneity, inequalities, diversities,
but not enmity among them. The modern spiritual environment seems to
need a revisiting of those themes that intimately concern every man within
his existential situation. Until recently the judgment that 'the reality which
we confront of a world without a God is partly the reaction to a God without

a world'[2] could have claimed some validity. But as we journey into the postmodern this kind of separation seems to have become more and more problematic.

This essay, while dealing mainly with philosophy, since he who writes is a philosopher, does not forget that faith, like reason, is a cognitive energy, not merely piety and obedience, as the critics of Christianity and Revelation, beginning with Spinoza, have implied. Our theme is philosophy in itself and in its relationship to a faith reaching for its self-understanding (*fides quaerens intellectum*): the energy of reason may imbue the comprehension of faith without changing it, while on the other hand the energy of faith issuing from Revelation may live within the heart of reason without violence and danger to it. On the contrary, faith may disclose to reason new horizons and endow it with something awesome. A passage from the book of Tobias, one of the most exquisite to be found in the Bible, comes to mind (cf. ch. 6). Faith can be for philosophy something analogous to what the archangel Rafael has been in Tobias' journey: he guided the journey, neutralized the marine monsters and prepared a collyrium to protect Tobias' eyes from diseases and strengthen their vision. In the encounter with philosophy, Revelation challenges it to be itself and to reach its full potential. In order for this to happen, it is first necessary to overcome the principle of immanence, one of the main heritages of rationalism and the hinge, at various stages of modernity, around which revolve the principal objections to the very idea of a Revelation. The criterion of immanence eliminates at its root any dialogue between man and Revelation. And once Revelation has been eliminated, what we are left with is a very powerful and solitary reason. It is a matter of urgency that the relation between philosophy and Revelation, between reason and faith, be thought out anew in the light of the new spiritual horizons of the postmodern era, of the uncertainties that distress the relationship, and of the question of meaning that runs through it.

Notes

1   A few months after the promulgation of the encyclical, we get the impression, which is obviously temporary and subject to a later revision, that its review within modern culture has been rather deficient and at times even prejudged. When the document first appeared, the Italian media hurried out a few on-the-spot articles with interviews of academicians who declared that they had no knowledge of the encyclical and that in any case they expected nothing from it. The few more thoughtful contributions, such as the one in *Micromega* (1998, n.5) give the impression that their purpose was that of contesting rather than understanding. In rare cases (and I am thinking here of the article by E. Scalfari in *La Repubblica* of 18 October 1998) one may gather that the document revolves around the theme of truth and knowledge and that the Pope may be right on at least one point: people cannot live without meaning in their lives.

2   W. Kasper, *Fede e storia*, Brescia: Queriniana, 1975, p.160.

Chapter 1

Philosophy of Being

The Responsibility of Philosophy

The relationship between religion and philosophy, faith and reason, is a multifaceted theme. Among the various points of departure we cannot leave out a sentence from the encyclical *Fides et Ratio* itself: 'Reason too needs to be sustained in all its search by trusting dialogue and sincere friendship. A climate of suspicion and distrust, which can beset theoretical research, ignores the teaching of the ancient philosophers who proposed friendship as one of the most appropriate contexts for sound philosophical enquiry' (n.33). Within the friendly camaraderie of those who search for the truth one may glimpse something of the fundamental friendship among the various forms of knowledge, to which we will allude later when dealing with the subject of wisdom and its home, which includes different floors. Those two types of friendships cannot be separated from one another.

But beyond such a fitting invitation, what does this encyclical mean for a philosopher? In the first place it introduces philosophy as the proper place wherein to listen to man's current difficulties, especially since it is exactly within philosophy that the question of truth and meaning is felt most intensely. It is within philosophical thought that the depths of our convictions are most authentically revealed. Tied to this notion is the idea that philosophical thought establishes a universal ground among cultures, under the aegis of some originative issues which can be found anew by any man in any era because they deal with the very enigma of his existence and the meaning of being. On these issues *Fides et Ratio* grounds its praise and positive pronouncement about philosophy, a praise that is hardly ever proffered nowadays by either individuals or by institutions. If we simply recall the sad condition of difficulty, abandonment and even, at times, exclusion wherein philosophy languishes within modern culture, then the philosophers will have reasons to be grateful for the homage paid to their discipline. The encyclical reminds us that man is naturally a philosopher (n.64); it presents philosophy as 'one of the noblest tasks of mankind' (n.3), it affirms that the Church 'sees in philosophy the way to come to know fundamental truths about man's existence' (n.5). It deplores the fact that philosophy has been made to assume an utterly marginal role (n.47) and that reason has been reduced to so-called 'weak reason' (n.48). As for the situation within the Church itself, the encyclical points out with disappointment that 'many Catholic faculties, after the Vatican II Council, were in some ways impoverished by a diminished sense of the importance of the study not just of Scholastic philosophy but more generally of the study of philosophy itself' (n.61).

And the document does not fail to remind philosophers of their responsibility in the matter: one should not get out of difficulties through a sort of philosophical wandering which may be brilliant but still intimates, more or less openly, a surrender of sorts. The purpose is to challenge, to encourage philosophy and not to bury it; there is a clear reminder to philosophy of its responsibility in an era when so many have proclaimed its death while privileging the natural and the human sciences. As the argument goes, these sciences have snatched from philosophy all of its prerogatives so that at the end of a centuries-long process philosophy is left without any object and its insistence on existing is an insistence on nothing.

Those times when Hegel, in line with the central presuppositions of his system, considered God the *one* and *only* object of philosophy, which was as such essentially theology and divine service, are long gone. Assuming that Hegel had it right, what ensues later is a secularization of philosophy placed at the service of the earthly and the finite, followed later by a deconstruction–dissolution according to which philosophy is now destined to vegetate unless it consents to becoming a mere reflection on scientific knowledge. These philosophical tendencies, recognizable in modern culture and its various branches of knowledge, lead to a necessary reflection on the consequences of the liquidation of philosophy, since without it meaning cannot easily be preserved. Ultimately what should be normative has to be borrowed from the highest spiritual levels: philosophy and theology. There is something strange in the fact that it is a man of faith, even a Pope, who credits reason and rehabilitates it. One can already hear those voices which, after identifying the Church as the mother of every obscurantism and irrationalism, will presently manifest their displeasure of the fact that she now accords too much importance and responsibility to reason.[1]

The first step of philosophy is not that of falling at faith's feet. Rather philosophy encounters faith, questions it and sometimes welcomes it, looking for understanding and cooperation. Ideally faith and philosophy should be friends, certainly different and heterogeneous but still friends, respecting and acquainted with each other. Even if pursued by different roads, their aim is the same: to know the truth and derive joy and satisfaction from it. The purpose of philosophy is that of knowing reality, knowing being, and ultimately God. Philosophy can grasp God's existence, know something about Him, even when it cannot reach Him: it is capable of looking at the transcendent even if it cannot lead us there. When philosophy reaches those heights it can have trust that from 'beyond this world' may come towards man a friendly power that may be of help on the journey. Be that as it may, philosophy can at least remain in an attitude of openness while waiting for an eventual ulteriority.

The horizon in which it behoves us to locate ourselves is that of philosophic reason willing to fully listen. *An open philosophy can be defined as one that, through a rational and verifiable procedure, acknowledges its own inadequacy in attaining a complete vision*; a philosophy, in other words, which discovers that it is inadequate and incomplete for the attainment of the fullness of truth and wisdom. Being aware of its limitations, this kind of philosophy has a natural propensity to integrate the elements reached by reason with those of faith. Naturally, this requires that theology also, as rational mediation of faith, assume an attitude of openness and readiness to be questioned and challenged by Revelation, by culture, by the events of history. In a more immediate sense, 'open philosophy' means something that does not place obstacles in the journey towards what is beyond the reach of reason. By itself it does not yet mean something that 'points towards', something that leads directly to faith. We know that within modernity the tension between faith and reason has been strained almost to the breaking point, with the danger that we will reach polar positions: either *sola fides* or *sola ratio*.[2] The request of the Church's magisterium is to be located with its originality within this framework. Whenever it has pronounced itself on philosophical matters (and it has done so often in the last 150 years), it has always avoided, despite the undisputed tensions, the breaking of the nexus between faith and reason. Faith has no interest in the discrediting of reason, as a problematic and rather superficial kind of apologetic may have claimed, and the critique that faith brings to enlightened and rationalistic reason has not surrendered to the other extreme position of a splendidly isolated faith erected on the ruins of any human research.

An attitude of openness and dialogue does not rob philosophy of its autonomy: it is nobody's *ancilla*. If it is true that for a long time complaints have been raised about those expressions implying that philosophy is to be considered the servant of theology (an improper expression since it fails to safeguard the basic autonomy of philosophical thinking), what we need to fear nowadays is that philosophy may have become *ancilla scientiarum*: increasingly the sciences are given the task of assigning to philosophy the very subjects on which it should think, the parameters within which to operate, the field of the objects to be investigated. While science may appear much more powerful than philosophy in its capacity to change life, its theories do not encompass the whole of reality as do those of philosophy, and they remain more uncertain and ever-changing when compared with the fundamental cognitive conquests of philosophy which reach sometimes the form of stable and undeniable knowledge. Science is not in a position to make transcendent choices horizontally or vertically; its method allows it to consider only the element of becoming, due to the fact that nature itself is constantly changing, with the corollary impossibility of ever reaching the level of the eternal and of the ultimate sense. Within those areas the encyclical declares itself a partner with that part of philosophy which offers an alternative to the central theme of the ancient and new positivism; that is, the idea that only science can reach knowledge and that, consequently, philosophy has at best the function of support for the sciences, a mere epistemological criterion to put its achievements in some order.

If we were to ask what it means to recall philosophy to its responsibilities, I would answer thus: philosophy should reconnect to and repeat the original experiences from which it issued. There are two great roots from which philosophy originated: the sense of *wonder* before being and life, and the sense of *reverence and awe*, understood not as fright or phobia, but as a meditative pause on that which ends and dies, on the falling away towards disappearance of things and of life itself.[3] Astonishment and wonder produce in us the desire to know and to philosophize; the same can be said for *meditatio mortis*. While in the Book of Proverbs and the Siracidae we read that '*Initium sapientiae timor Domini*', at least a part of philosophy could well say that '*Initium philosophiae meditatio mortis*'. Here philosophy shows its essential vocation to function as an antidote to the horrors of meaninglessness, and perhaps as a preparation for an existence that is more free than the earthly one. And yet, philosophy having for a long time pronounced so much on death, especially on its nexus to immortality, in today's significant spiritual transformation the issue of death is largely assigned to the sciences. When science evaluates death with its own methodology it understands it as a mere biological fact that does not point to any ulterior question. It finds it futile to contemplate any substantial difference between the disappearance of man and that of any other living being. We keep hearing 'One dies and that's all', but there is also afloat a tendency to assign mortality to everything that exists. *The whole is mortal*. The *meditatio mortis* does not seem to concern philosophy any longer. Within philosophical schools there is a preference for logical, formal, epistemological matters which, while important in their own right, are nevertheless diverging from the seriousness of the issue of death. This group of issues constitutes an impoverishment, with the consequent loss of a powerful incentive to thinking.

The act of philosophizing is in danger whenever man stops feeling wonder before being, the kind of wonder which moves something deep within him; or else when he stops feeling the challenge of the absurd originating from the certainty of having to die. Those two branches of philosophizing were well known to the ancients. It would be enough to remember Aristotle and above all Plato who, in the *Phaedo*, understands philosophy as *meditatio/praeparatio mortis*.[4] Whenever wonder before being and life – which abound and constantly give of themselves – is scarce, whenever *meditatio mortis* is no longer practised, we have good motives to suspect that human reason has become anaemic and lazy. That kind of 'weak reason', so much in vogue nowadays, may turn out to be a tired reason, unfit for new explorations of the essential experiences of existence regarding life and death.

The Issue of Truth

The fundamental problem of our era, as of any other era, is that of truth. The issue must be framed within the present conditions of spiritual existence within which the rationalism of past centuries, over-confident of its ability to reach truth, has now been superseded by a radical mistrust of reason. We have here the drama of worldwide philosophical thinking which at times even attempts to eliminate the very idea of truth. Strategically, the encyclical presents man as 'the one who seeks the truth' (n.28). If we attempt to understand this statement, we must say that human reason, with an incoercible power issuing from a natural inclination set within the dynamics of the human faculties and preceding the act of free will, is by its own nature bent towards the truth. That is to say, every man naturally desires to know, and to know the truth, not falsehood; so that, in the dualities 'knowledge–knowledge of truth', and 'search–search for truth', the second term does nothing but explain what is already implicit in the first. What is being introduced with those premises is a nearly new definition of man to be placed next to the more traditional definitions such as *animal rationale*, or *animal liberum*.

Thus we have the premise to uphold an ontological priority, or the primacy of truth over freedom: the mind cleanses itself with truth and the intellect with knowledge. Within this idea that man is structurally and essentially he who searches for the truth, there is something that transcends it: the assumption that his destiny – whatever it may be – is to be considered fulfilled or lost, depending on whether or not he is in a position to reach a personal relationship with truth. Within this conception of man the existential appropriation of truth is decisive. Here lies an important problematic, that of going beyond abstract norms and of preferring and following the living example of a sage master.

The very destiny of philosophy is played out within the space of truth which finds its most qualified level in metaphysics: beyond the legitimate variations of the schools of thought, *metaphysics can be defined as the search by the intellect for the clarification of the structure of the whole*, or even the search on the mystery of everything there is in order to arrive at a stable knowledge. By adopting the term 'mystery' rather than the more normal 'problem' we intimate that mystery is different from the absurd: there is no equivalency between the two, as rationalism has sustained and still sustains. Mystery, far from constituting a contradiction or a destitution of reason, is rather a fullness of truth, a truth that is veiled, in the shadows, inexhaustible, within which the mind wanders without being able to grasp it fully, but at the same time getting confirmation of an original intuition on the unconditional nature and the universality of truth. This capacity for truth of human reason is given testimony not only by some universal cognitions such as those expressed in first speculative and moral principles, but also by the progressive encounter of man with truth throughout history, an encounter that takes place as man opens himself to being, and realized as the soul expands and knowledge develops. All of these attainments find their culmination in the knowledge of God as final destination and as the completion of every kind of knowledge. These very assumptions are criticized and even rejected nowadays by a mistrustful attitude and an all-pervading scepticism which deprive human reason of its 'theo-relative' capacity, that is directed and referring to God.

The ascertaining of the truth of being is the task of the speculative *Standpunkt* wherein the sense of the whole is not decided but unveiled: we need to let being be, we need to let it appear. Strictly related to the issue of a theoretical look at the whole of reality is the counterpoint theme of the forgetfulness of being. Although this term is Heidegerrian in origin, and therefore tied to an ambiguous mode of introducing the issue of 'ontological difference', there is no reason why we should understand it only in a

Heideggerian mode. It is my view that forgetfulness of being means that, for part of postmodern culture, being and existence are silent, not revelatory: being is not 'phanic' or revealing (even under the aspect of symbolism), because it is mere *res extensa* revealing nothing. Within this condition, which is both cultural and existential, reality will appear to the subject as something foreign, hostile: consequently the relation to it can be thought of only in the form of challenge and domination. The issue of truth as an unveiling (*aletheia*) remains central for both philosophy and theology since, besides a divine Revelation, there exists also a natural word, a revelatory natural attitude of being; in as much as it is phanic it is also theophanic, or God revealing. Metaphysical research is tied to this natural unveiling. The encounter between believing thought and postmodernity could never happen outside this dimension.

This core issue is one and the same as the issue of truth and meaning. Although the encyclical's title bears the terms 'faith' and 'reason' – long consecrated by tradition, even when the tendency is to suppress or oppose one to the other – its subject matter is not that as much as the issue of truth (cf. the beginning: 'Faith and reason are like two wings on which the human spirit rises to the contemplation of truth') and Revelation ('Underlying all the Church's thinking is the awareness that she is the bearer of a message which has its origin in God himself': n.7). Those two elements (truth and Revelation) on which the encyclical reflects seem to be the two foci of a document which aims at returning to an original nexus between faith and reason; one that in the past has produced abundant fruits in Western thought.

It would be symptomatic of superficiality to interpret the title of the encyclical as if it declared that faith and reason were respectively identical to theology and philosophy. The intentional–cognitive act of reason and the event of Revelation are more originative; in other words, they precede both a technically structured philosophy and a faith searching for self-knowledge through theology. The dialogue between Revelation, the Bible, reason, philosophy and faith happens and must be thought out within history, but not in such a way that its result is fully resolved within the circle of historicity. The word enunciated by reason and the word listened to by faith are not to be reduced to a mere historic–cultural context, as a radical multiculturalism and contextualism assumes nowadays. On the other hand, the postulate of the unity of truth intimated by the image of the two wings with which the human spirit soars toward truth does not contradict the usual experience of the fragmentation of truth into a multiplicity of partial truths, as long as one admits that the fullness of truth is eschatological. That postulate, however, remains important as a guide within dispersion.

If the theme is truth as reached by philosophy and donated by faith – since a claim to truth is intrinsic to the very act of faith – then we need to distance ourselves from the diagnosis which announces the end of metaphysics and from the mistrust of reason declared by this position. We must distance ourselves from the oblivion of being, and its strictly related anti-realism which are found within 'weak thought' as well as in a constructivism which conceives of the object as a construction of the subject. This assumption seems present in various versions of science, especially in the human ones. Although the term 'realism' is rarely used in the encyclical, the idea of real and objective knowledge which it implies is found everywhere in the papal Letter, to the point of establishing a fundamental presupposition according to which not only the sciences but philosophy and faith also are capable of knowledge.

The Concept of Truth as Conformity

Through the issue of real knowledge the determination of the essence of (declarative) truth is then approached according to the formula – itself universal and incontrovertible, hence adopted surreptitiously by the very people who would like to deny it – of *adaequatio intellectus et rei*, that is the conformity between the mind and the things it apprehends. The encyclical deals with this issue in its essential unity (cf. nn. 56, 82) by rejecting any attempt to make a dualism of the very concept of truth by fitting one for the hermeneutical sciences and another for the sciences of nature (the first characterized by the 'truth' of understanding and interpretation, the other by the 'method' of verification as Gadamer understands it to a certain extent). The concept of realism (here we will refer to the moderate realism) means that all the light comes from the being, from the object, so that the process of knowing is not a creative act of the mind and not even in primary meaning an interpretative or hermeneutical act, but a perceptive one. Although 'realism' comes from *res*, it would be a deep misunderstanding (not infrequent, however) to put an identity between realism and 'thingism' (*chosisme, cosismo*), where 'thingism' would be a doctrine of knowledge which takes into account only things which can be seen and touched. Realism is not 'thingism' because the term *res* in the classical formula on declarative truth is a transcendental notion, which as such applies to any form of reality and existence, not only to physical things.

In its synthetic power the concept of truth as conformity or correspondence between the cognitive act of the subject and reality embraces any possible level of knowledge and goes even beyond the fundamental level of declarative or theoretical truth, applying it even to the moment of moral action and to that of following a master, where one would act to 'make true' something. In the practical truth, conformity is to be understood as the conformity of the right desire (and of the will) to law: it is not superfluous to recall that according to Kant the good and the evil, that is the moral truth, are the conformity (or its contrary) of the will in respect of the law (see the first chapter of *Die Religion innerhalb der Grenzen der blossen Vernunft*). In following a master, a typical case being that of religious experience, truth appears as something or someone to whom one gives witness, making one's own life conform to what is asked and/or to a living example.

This concept remains normative for every kind of knowledge, even if the attempt to abandon the determination of the *adaequatio* may have contaminated some recent expressions of philosophy and theology. In such a case, those who see a radical hermeneutics (which rejects precisely the *adaequatio*) as a mode of thought which is friendly towards religion would be right. Nevertheless, even if we grant that eliminating the idea of truth as conformity may also eliminate the negations of religion, what results is that religion is placed under the same standard as any other element of reality and then one arrives at a radical relativism wherein everything may be equally true and equally false. In fact the very assertion that 'everything is false' is true.[5]

It is not superfluous to add here that, regarding the issue of truth, we have seen explicit challenges in the first reactions to *Fides et Ratio*. They are introduced with the assertion that we do not need any ultimate truths, maintaining in fact that the renunciation of metaphysics as the place where one knows what meaning is constitutes a victory for postmodern reason. Wherever there has been criticism or rejection, the motive can be traced back, not so much to the missing link between faith and reason (hence not in the position of only faith or only reason), as to the issue of reason as such, which is to say to the issue of truth and meaning. Regarding this issue some have said or will continue to say: 'We know quite well that there is no truth or meaning in life and Being. We ourselves create meaning in a way that we may go on living.' From this attempt of man to create his own meaning one derives, on the one hand, the success of subjectivity closed upon itself and wanting to extract everything from itself, and on the other hand the eclipse of the revelatory and phanic character of being. On this last aspect we meet nowadays the powerful influence of the spirit of domination of technology and the related primacy of instrumental reason over revelatory reason. With the ushering in of instrumental reason there occurs a change in the very perception of being and the orders and ranks that are internal to it: being in its highest meaning does not consist any longer in *being always*, but in remaining in the presence of, ready for any transformation and disappearance. Therefore being in its highest meaning would consist of a being ready to vanish, to extinguish itself, to be-for-death.

As elaborated by philosophic thought, the doctrine of truth as conformity has found supporters within science which is permeated by a thrust towards reality. Copernicus, Kepler, Galileo, Newton, Leibniz and many others were persuaded that the laws they discovered corresponded to the nature of things, that to some extent they expressed the world's intelligibility, and that even granting that the researcher searched for an answer, it was nature itself that spoke. In order to get to the theory of general relativity, Einstein calculated the movement of Mercury, thus discovering that the new theory explained with accuracy an anomaly in the Newtonian theory which had perplexed astronomers.

Although the idea of truth as conformity can be understood in various modes, some of them are merely formal modes which invalidate its realistic value. Within modernity, various objections have been moved against the idea of truth, beginning with Descartes and Spinoza. One of those objections, which ends up dissolving the very realistic concept of truth, is the Spinozian assumption according to which the veritative relationship is established between the idea and its mental construct; the idea is considered true in itself by its own perfection and not because of a correspondence with the thing. Thus the causal relationship of truth is turned upside-down, in the sense that its conformity with reality derives from the truth of the idea. Since it is not conformity that establishes the truth of the idea, the form of true thought is to be sought within thought itself and is to be deduced from the nature of the intellect. Idealism will pick up those concepts and give them a final form, as one can gather from Schelling's early thought (*System of Transcendental Idealism*, 1800) and from Hegel (*The Science of Logic*).

On the other hand, the concept truth as correspondence in its realistic meaning has been taken up again in the 19th century and in the 20th century by thinkers such as Bolzano and Meinong, from positivism and from a series of Thomistic philosophers (Gilson, Maritain, Fabro, Lonergan). In 20th-century thought we detect a substantial acceptance of the idea of truth as conformity or correspondence by scientists and philosophers not touched by deconstructive deviations, among whom especially Popper and Tarski. They recognize as valid the idea of truth as correspondence, although Popper (cf. *Objective Knowledge, Research without End*, nn.20, 32) is more sensitive towards the realistic element which it implies, while the other with its semantic theory ends up reducing correspondence to formalized languages. The Popperian reintroduction of the concept of truth as correspondence, even if in the long run, was required from the theory of fallibilism. Such a term would have no sense unless one presupposes that the scientific theory which has been disproved by facts is not in conformity with the real. This implies that fallibilism, rather than being understood, as it could be, as the threshold to scepticism, is rather a sort of 'meliorism' (as was understood by Peirce).

Even the hermeneutical positions, if one considers them carefully, come close, at least formally, to truth as conformity, which in their case consists in the conformity of the interpretation to what is interpreted, even though such a correspondence is often considered unreachable. Ultimately within truth as interpretation the focus falls on the hermeneutical character of our experience of the world. In this regard we may mention Betti's positions (*Teoria dell'interpretazione*, 1955) and those of Pareyson (*Teoria e interpretazione,* 1971), according to which the unitary and identical truth incarnates and expresses itself in multiple historical formulations, which represent the temporal arrival of the atemporal and unique truth. According to Ricoeur (*Le conflit des interprétations*, 1969) the same diversity of interpretations which continually arise implies a going back to something that could put an end to it. On the other hand, the position of radical and deconstructive hermeneutics such as Deridda's denies any form of hermeneutical objectivity and Vattimo (*Oltre l'interpretazione*, 1994) transforms truth as conformity to truth as openness understood as a metaphor for dwelling. The danger of a metaphorical dissolution of the very concept of truth is quite high.

Fides et Ratio, in suggesting the concept of truth as conformity or correspondence, places itself at a decisive watershed, in the sense that, in determining declarative truth as correspondence, it takes its distances from the other alternate concepts of truth that have arisen within philosophy: that is to say, the concept of truth as *coherence*, that of *intersubjective consensus* and that according to which truth is to be found within *efficiency* and *utility*. The first is Kant's; the second is nowadays defended by many authors who generally belong in one way or another to the Kantian genealogy mediated by *linguistic turn* (Apel, Habermas and so on); the third was adopted by Nietzsche and in other aspects from Pragmatism (W. James, Dewey, and partly by Peirce). It now behoves us to analyse these concepts of truth.

Different Concepts of Truth

1   Truth as coherence is to be found in critical philosophy. In Kantian thought we still find truth as conformity, intended however as a mere *nominal* definition introducing the *formal* criterion of truth as coherence of thought with itself, understood as the agreement of thought with the general necessary laws of the intellect. Kant asserts that 'What contradicts those laws, is false because in such a case the intellect is opposed to its own laws, that is to say, to itself.'[6] By accepting and assuming 'the nominal definition of truth as agreement of a knowing subject with its own object', Kant observes in this work that 'the purely logical criterion of truth, that is to say the agreement of the knowing subject with the general and formal laws of the intellect and of reason, is the *conditio sine qua non*, and therefore the negative condition of every truth', which then needs to take the next step to transcendental logic which is capable of exposing the elements of the pure knowledge of the intellect as well as the principles without which no object can ever be thought: it is a logic of truth.[7]

Within such a stance, truth is the agreement of one proposition with the system of the other propositions; that is to say, the agreement or conformity of propositions among themselves rather than with reality. This results in the greatest success of antirealism and is part of the Kantian problematic idea of the thing in itself (the noumenon), which will eventually be sarcastically derided by Hegel in his *Science of Logic*. By criticizing the separation of thought from being introduced by Kant, and which is the origin of a great many equivocations on the problem of truth, Hegel tries to arrive at an idea of logic not as formal science but as science of truth, by identifying the rational with the real.

It is possible, however, to distinguish formal truth from material truth: the first kind of truth would consist of a non-contradiction and a logical coherence of deductions issuing out of premises or postulates; the other would consist of agreement with reality. The assertions of pure geometry are true if they are coherent with axioms which are conventionally postulated at the beginning. However, merely formal truth is not enough, since any relationship with reality has been eliminated from it. It needs to be integrated with material truth, understood at a minimum as a compatibility with assertions expressing empirical facts. In this regard, Schlick wrote: 'I see no obstacle – in fact I consider it normal – to use the good old expression "conformity with reality" for this kind of compatibility.'[8] On the contrary, the neopositivism of Carnap and of Neurath understood truth as an internal coherence among propositions, a theory that Schlick considered completely inadequate.[9] In fact, the theory of truth as coherence does not furnish any univocal criterion of truth, since it is logically possible to arrive at any number of systems of propositions internally non-contradictory, and yet externally, or in respect of reality, quite incompatible, thus arriving at the idea not of the double truth but of the multiple truth.

2   Truth as intersubjective consensus, which adds to truth as coherence a search for intersubjectivity, is held by the recent philosophies of communication (Apel, Habermas). They search for an intersubjective of consensus which is ideally unlimited and which could be understood as a further form of truth as coherence. In this case it would be seen as a coherence of the discourse with itself in which the reference to the *res* disappears, or as an asymptotic conformity with reality, wherein the meaning of truth as correspondence would be recovered. For these authors truth is either an assumption, so that he who speaks and argues implies among the conditions of his discourse truth and truthfulness, or the final goal of the unlimited communicative act within the community: that of reaching a convergent point of our beliefs. It remains unclear whether the consensus sought is only a linguistic intersubjective one or a real objective one; that is, one based on a real effective conformity with being. Another notable question concerns the extension of the unlimited community of communication: does it include the transcendent, or does it in principle simply operate a limitation to the human world and the dialogue among men? One of the risks of the doctrine of truth as intersubjectivity is that of identifying intersubjective knowledge as the only valid knowledge. On the other hand, Wittgenstein's idea according to which we cannot get out of language is not in itself opposed to the doctrine of conformity, if we understand conformity as the correspondence of a proposition with something which can be expressed through language and that reaches the *res* through language.

With truth as coherence in an open mode, and within truth as intersubjectivity in an unstable mode, the reference to empirical reality is intentionally truncated: hence the idea of truth as intersubjectivity can be near or far from that of truth as conformity. When near, the idea of conformity remains under a disguise of sort, expressed as an asymptotic conformity in the long run. While it is the case that, using the criterion of truth as coherence, one can construct an unlimited number of propositional systems that do not impinge on reality, with the criterion of intersubjective truth one can construct within science a propositional system which gives man power over nature and where disagreement is rare.

3   The determination of truth as effectiveness is developed along two analogous, but not identical, lines: the line of truth as utility for life, and the line wherein truth explicates an instrumental and operative effectiveness. The first idea was proposed by Nietzsche for whom truth is what results as useful for life. Nietzsche will assert, 'the falsehood of a judgment is still not for us an objection to it'.[10] For this author truth is not something that exists and needs to be discovered, but rather something to be created for the enhancement of life.

W. James, without connecting his thought to that of Nietzsche, spread with his pragmatism the idea that, within the field of morality and religion, truth is to be found in its capacity to offer efficacious solutions to life's problems. Others amplified the scope of this idea, considering true everything that might increase through knowledge man's dominion over the cosmos, or what might morally improve human relations. Dewey's pragmatism has analogous but not identical characteristics, in the sense that it tends to underline the pragmatic and operational capacity of multiple cognitive procedures which possess truth, that is to say effectiveness in the modification of nature and society. Dewey takes his bearing from a sort of operational instrumentalism, in the sense that the same operation of thinking is an action whose purpose is to modify and change the conditions under which objects present themselves. Hence concepts are instruments with which we think the objects and with which we change their conditions (cf. *Renewing Philosophy*, 1919).

Relational Structure of the Concept of Truth

One of the greatest problems of modernity, already present in Descartes, was clearly formulated by Kant, who considered it vital as well as difficult to solve: how something within the mind can be the representation of something outside the mind.[11] This is the problem of *intentionality* and of the *concept* which is evoked, since intentionality should be understood at least as the original phenomenon which relates thought and being, mind and world. Modern philosophy has been deeply affected by this problem, whose unclear or failed solution has had many decisive consequences, among which the attempt at transforming the very concept of truth.

As we meditate on the question of truth, which is characterized by a large polysemy of its concept, a necessary step is that of determining the distinct modalities of 'something being true'. First, there is the modality represented by the very existence of things. Things are as they are; they are true: *verum est id quod est*, Augustine would write (*Soliloquia*, 1: II, c.5). Truth is reality: it resides in its sovereign and proud indifference; it keeps its secret. We are the ones who question it. We call 'ontological truth' this modality of true being. The place of this kind of truth are things themselves, according to the degree/level of being of each of them: 'Each thing possesses so much of truth as much of being' (*Metaphysics*: 993, b, 30).

The second modality is that of declarative truth, which expresses itself in and by judgment, and which assumes the form of conformity between judgment and reality (*adaequatio intellectus et rei*). This level of truth can be called 'declarative truth' or 'logical truth'. The place of this truth is the mind, in the sense that it is the act of the mind which, by conforming or not conforming itself to reality, renders thought either true or false. In this kind of modality truth is the relation of the intellect to the thing inasmuch as it is knowable.

The third modality is that by which the idea is expressed that things, being what they are, always point to the creative intellect (or to a human creator), on which they depend for their position within being. Since here truth is the relationship to a thought (in the hypothesis of a universe without thought, we would have existence but not truth), for truth to exist there must be a thought that thinks it. The first level is oriented to and is fulfilled in the third level, which can be given the name of 'absolute ontological truth'. Even in this modality the determination of truth as conformity (*adaequatio*) – which is two-faced and which in the present instance is understood as the conformity of the thing to the intellect that posits it and that maintains it into existence (not as *adaequatio intellectus et rei*, but as *adaequatio rei et intellectus*) – remains valid.

In the second and third determination the concept of truth shows an intrinsic relational structure: it declares a relationship between thought and being, intellect and object. The formula which expresses 'logical' truth as conformity (*adaequatio intellectus et rei*) shows by its very linguistic and semantic structure the nature of truth as relationship between thought (*intellectus*) and being (*res*), between the intelligibility of being and the intentional opening of the intellect. There is truth where there is thought. In a cosmos without any form of thinking there would not be any declarative truth, for there would not be any thought to express it.

Since declarative truth is a relation, the understanding of the concept of truth will change according to the conception one has of the two poles of the relationship. Within the postmodern, the critique is on the side of the mind, with emphasis put on the crisis or the death of reason, considered inadequate for grasping reality or life. In philosophies of Cartesian or rationalistic derivations, equivocations arise and spread from the understanding of being (the *res*): being or the *res* are understood in an immanent mode as the idea or the represented object, and on the basis of this assumption the problem of how the mental idea can represent reality becomes insoluble (a question which is solved in the classical position where ideas and concepts do not *represent* but directly *present* the object). Following this road, one ends up conceiving of truth as the relation between the thinking subject and the interior fruit of its thinking activity, and therefore in the final analysis as the *coherence of thought with itself*. It is finally worth remembering that the act of conformity of the mind to being requires a profound and actual involvement of the whole person. This position refutes what is sometimes attributed to the doctrine of truth as conformity: that it does not pay enough attention to the subject.

Within the doctrines which abandon truth as conformity one can detect an inability to comprehend or an unjustified reduction of the concept of *res*. Within empiricism the *res* is only what is sensible, what can be seen and touched. The accusation of naturalism, which some sectors of theology foreign to empiricism level against the concept of truth as conformity, is traceable to the equivocation which identifies *res* with material thing without taking into account the transcendental meaning of *res*. Within coherentism the *res* is no longer there, and truth is no longer a relation with otherness but a mere internal coherence, of a logical kind. In truth as intersubjectivity also, the *res* does not appear to interest much, or it is interesting only as an asymptotic correlate of a system of assertions.

The idea of truth as conformity is homogeneous with three assumptions which constitute central places of gnoseology and metaphysics. This means that its best comprehension requires that it be thought together with them; that is to say, with *moderate realism*, the possibility of *intellectual intuition* and the capital doctrine of the *intentional identity between thought and being*.[12] Unfortunately these three central points are often either not known or ignored by many doctrines of truth. As for the first aspect, we should keep in mind that moderate realism (Aristotle, Aquinas, Maritain) is different from the metaphysical realism of Putnam inasmuch as it does not assume a position from 'the eye of God', as Putnam defines it, not without serious equivocations. It should also be noted here that various Anglo-Saxon authors, such as Dummett and Quine, offer an analysis of the theme of realism that leaves much to be desired, since they are silent on moderate realism, perhaps wrongly confused with its 'absolute' rendering of Platonic origin.[13]

The second and third points represent the kernel of the gnoseology of the philosophy of being which has become lost within modern philosophy under two aspects: that of the refusal of intellectual intuition and that of a dualistic assumption according to which there exists an insurmountable barrier between thought and being. These equivocations, which are massively present in the work of Kant, are then proliferated through analytic philosophy, and their residue is to be found in post-Popperian and post-empirical epistemologies as an anti-realism which tends to increase (cf. Quine) and tends to lose even that reduced element of realism which could still be found in logical empiricism through the focusing on sensible perception. For all those reasons it is futile to hope that those above-mentioned schools may effectively recover the doctrine of truth as conformity, capable of going beyond the nominal or verbal acceptance of the consecrated formula, given the fact that the very suppositions of ontological and gnoseological order, which made it true, valid and live, have been lost.

This kind of equivocation can also be found within the philosophies of communication: see, for example, the vast study of Apel on 'Fallibilism, theory of truth as consensus and ultimate foundation'.[14] This author does not completely reject the concept of truth as conformity, which he in fact retains as necessary and coherent with common sense: one cannot doubt that the assertion 'the wall is white' is true if, and only if, the wall is in fact white. But the concept is rendered invalid since Apel cannot find criteria of truth which would allow the verification of conformity. Apelian aporetic is developed between two poles: that in which it is recognized that the theory of truth as correspondence is a natural intuition on the truth of what is enunciated, and is hence 'assumed as necessary condition of all theories of truth',[15] and the pole wherein truth as conformity is rejected as formal and empty. Apel remains within Kantian dualism, since he is unable to recover the doctrine of intentional identity between thought and being, no hint of which can be discerned. Consequently the acceptance by Apel of the Kantian assumption of a separation between thought and being transforms the concept of truth from a relation between mind and things, which is to say between subject and objects, into a relation among objects; in this relation, which lacks a superior point of observation, it would never be possible to verify the correspondence of thought to reality.

This is not a surprising result, once one has assumed the absolute exteriority between thought and being. Following this line of thought, Apel ends up asserting the inversion of the relationship between facts and propositions ('the concept of *fact* or of *existent state of things* is definable in turn only by referring to the concept of *true proposition*', p.95) and even abandoning the inferential argument which goes from the empirical evidence to its causes (inferential or analytical method which proceeds from the effects to the causes). The question as to whether the intersubjective consensus depends on the truth of judgment, or vice versa if it is the truth that founds itself on consensus, remains unanswered. All valid knowledge has the capacity to produce consensus, but it is not the consensus which founds it. (Some deeper insights on the concept of truth in three great thinkers of the 20th century, Maritain, Wittgenstein and Heidegger, are developed in Annex I.)

The Issue of Freedom

If, according to Heidegger, the essence of truth is freedom,[16] we should not be too surprised if, to the forgetfulness of being and truth, is added that of freedom, understood at least as an impoverishment of the idea of freedom and of the extension of its concept. To this matter is related the delicate nexus between freedom and truth, the very crux of many dramatically debated issues. We know that the problem of freedom constitutes one of the most crucial problematics of modernity, perhaps its central agenda from Descartes to Fichte and Schelling, from Kant to Bergson and Sartre. At the same time it constitutes one of the still unresolved heritages of the transition from the modern to the postmodern, especially when dealing with the question of whether or not freedom constitutes that primaeval basis no longer granted to being. With the ensuing crisis of speculative reason and its attempts to gain from the side of freedom what is lacking on the side of truth, the issue assumes even more urgency.

Two conditions are necessary to think through the problematic of freedom successfully, with the corollary quest to determine whether they occur within postmodernity. The first condition is an adequate anthropological philosophy capable of demonstrating sufficient introspection as regards the origin within man of the act of freedom and what is the relationship to it of the faculties of will and intelligence. The second condition has to do with ascertaining the semantic extension and the depths of the content of such a concept, which is often superficially assimilated or even identified with the concept of freedom of choice.

The issue of freedom is much deeper than simple free will; nor can it be identified with mere autodetermination: besides freedom of choice (that 'pro-choice' on which much emphasis is placed by modern liberalism and which is aimed at the voter or the consumer), we ought to consider liberation in its social or spiritual form, which is such because it is constituted by freedom of autonomy, of spontaneity, of flourishing, of exultation. The issue goes even beyond that of mere praxis. It is important to remember here that it also encompasses the intellect. There is such a thing as *intellectual freedom* which is much more than mere freedom of thought as a civil right: the deepest essence of intellectual freedom consists in being faithful to being, in submitting to the object by respecting its exigencies. In this attitude the mind accomplishes a kind of freedom of spontaneity in the drive towards reality. Authentic intellectual freedom is an aspect of the problem of truth and goes in tandem with realism within a fruitful relationship between being and Revelation.

In Judaeo-Christian thought we meet a characteristic reference to the nexus between freedom and truth, a sort of pre-eminence and deeper influence of truth vis-à-vis freedom, or at least of anteriority of veritative reason as custodian and protector of meaning, history and life. This is an assumption which contrasts to some extent with the present postmodern emphasis on freedom. One of the most striking expressions to be found in the Gospels, which carries a teaching of Jesus, goes like this: 'You shall know the truth and the truth shall make you free' (John 8:32). Free from what? From the evil of guilt or – to use a theological term – from sin? Undoubtedly such an idea is part of the Gospel logion, but it is more than that, since it alludes to freedom as the fullness of liberation. According to the Gospels, freedom and liberation are a fruit that matures under the sun of truth. Therefore there seems to be a natural priority of truth over and above freedom, without forgetting that their dialogue happens within a virtuous circle wherein reason opening up to being aims at truth, and freedom predisposes itself to goodness. Part of present-day modern culture will sneer at this in perplexity. Such a culture is predisposed to turn the assumption upside-down, claiming that 'You will practise freedom and freedom will make you true.' This seems to be the formula of a new secularized canon where the primacy is attributed to freedom. Were we to consider only civil life, this unlimited affirmation of freedom is the source of a multitude of stances which renders the state ungovernable and the creation of a just society impossible.

This great confidence in freedom is a spiritual event that begs for some reflection. It is exactly when there is abroad a mistrust of truth resembling an acute scepticism and a universal *desperatio de veritate*, which is the most disturbing of guests knocking at the door and the terminal result of nihilism, that freedom is apotheosized. Let me here hasten to add that there is no doubt that every man wants freedom. But it is just as valid to affirm that every man wants to know the truth and not error. Within the nexus truth–freedom there is a priority of truth, in the sense that freedom by itself does not constitute truth; freedom can know and 'realize' truth, making it part of its practice. These affirmations should not be taken in an intellectualistic sense, since the action of a subject may spring from a love for the good reached in a non-intellectual mode. But even there it is truth that will inspire and attract the action for good.

If we were to see faith and reason as two paths leading to the knowledge of truth, then competition on principle between them, which is possible if we consider them as opposites, disappears. Competition means that what is attributed to one is subtracted from the other: if one gains, the other loses. Rationalism and atheism have thus perceived the nexus man–God: the more man elevates God, the more something essential is subtracted from man and he estranges himself from himself. The same pattern can be discerned in determining relations between human created freedom and uncreated divine freedom. For rationalism what is granted to one is subtracted from the other. The idea that the two freedoms may cooperate in the production of the good is not accepted. That is to say, according to this 'cooperative solution', the divine freedom acts as first cause and human freedom as secondary cause, so that a good action issues completely from God as first cause and completely from man as secondary cause.

The Paradigm of Reason and the Problem of Wisdom

Between the non-hostile difference between the word of reason and the word of Revelation we may ask what is the profile of the first one that emerges from the encyclical. It is an open, flexible reason capable of knowledge, far from the forgetfulness of being and therefore contemplative and wise, capable of 'seeing' and 'listening'; a strong reason which is not synonymous with proud, hard or hostile, but rather one trained by the experience of the human, one that knows compassion and pain. It is a reason shaped by experience, appropriating a doctrine of knowledge similar to that present in the 'Wisdom Books' of the Bible (we will return to this later), and capable of picking up fragments of eternity, in some cases to arrive at a stable kind of knowledge. It is a reason that is attentive to what is happening around it, that does not repeat the refrain heard in so much of today's philosophy, always ready to affirm that 'it is no longer possible nowadays that ...'. For example, metaphysics is no longer possible; or direct knowledge, rather than an interpretative one, is no longer possible; or today it is only possible to criticize, never to ground, and so on.

It should be stated at the outset that the paradigm of reason that is drawn in the document is of a metaphysical and contemplative kind, one that is considered more complete than mere ethical reason. It does not exclude hermeneutics, but it does not understand it as operating without an ontological underpinning which understands that human nature or human essence is basically unchanging in its desires, passions and necessities. Without such an assumption, the attempt to understand remote texts would be self-defeating; with the passage of time the subject would be different and so would be the minimum conditions necessary to understand them. In the forgetfulness and the eventual negation of essences one can identify one of the most dangerous configurations of nihilism. We say dangerous because without essences, and without a hierarchy of essences, we will never know on what to base the eventual respect due to the individuals that participate in those essences. Jonas has with reason written that '"essentialism" is not as easy to get rid of as the existentialism of a vulgar kind would like us to believe'.[17] The encyclical situates itself within this area of thought not only when it asks us to leave phenomenon and opt for grounding, but also when it encourages philosophical thought to aim for the essences.

The above mention of the 'Wisdom Books' deserves an elaboration. If we consider in a special way the *Qohelet* (or *Ecclesiastes*), we will notice in it an intense recalling of experience as the mode of investigation adequate for the discovery of reality and truth. The wise person of the *Qohelet* sees, experiences, compares, reflects and concludes. He may appear disappointed, disenchanted, even bitter. But he remains a sage who in his search for the knowledge and meaning of life does not cease to be a believer. His is also a painful kind of knowledge, because many things remain incomprehensible and full of injustice; it is moreover a kind of knowledge that protests vigorously so many certitudes, more astute and even more ferocious in its criticism than that of many present-day fallibilists and cynics. Various exegetes assert that in the *Qohelet* we have an original synthesis of reason and faith, of experience and revelation, since its protagonist remains a sage of Israel who keeps on looking for God despite the fact that he does not understand His ways and the way He relates to man. One lesson we can derive from the *Qohelet* is that, even after we grant the obscurity afflicting human life, there is no opposition in principle between wisdom and history as it is sustained by philosophies which opt for formal expressions of rationality. It can even be claimed that the author's reason, which is strongly rooted within experience, is autonomous or *juxta propria principia*, not self-sufficient, if by this term we mean the preliminary refusal of all other relationships and the entrenching of reason within itself.[18]

In the second place, *Fides et Ratio* introduces not a univocal but a polyvalent paradigm of reason: just as being can be expressed in many ways without ending up in pure equivocation, so can reason (*logos pollakos legetai*). We thus considerably enlarge the usual model of Western reason, often determined from the practices of science and from rationalism, even today when rationalism has much less self-confidence and scientific knowledge is perceived as precarious, standing on stilts, so to speak. And yet there exists a different outlook from the objectifying scientific one; there are forms of rationality that are different from the scientific one. The encyclical enlarges the picture with a plethora of references to Greek thought, to the Biblical and Hebrew world, and even with references to the Orient. This suggests a corollary consideration: that the prevalent model of reason within Western culture is rather tired: the drive towards existence seems to be on the decline despite the fact that everything we know is ultimately knowledge of being. I assume as quite plausible that the current crisis of truth and the ultimate issue of *desperatio de veritate* spring from an anaemic, formal and weak model of reason. When this type of reason confronts Christianity, it has difficulty in perceiving in it something more than an ethic. At that point two distractions ensue: that before being and that before the Christian phenomenon perceived as mere moral teaching, as by Kant. His major work of the philosophy of religion, *Die Religion innerhalb der Grenzen der blossen Vernunft*, is an explicit attempt to pour the new wine of Christianity into the old, chapped jars of mere morality. It is an attempt to fence in Christianity in order to domesticate the Incarnation, the Cross and the Resurrection by depriving them of their divine and salvific meaning and reducing them exclusively to the realm of morality.

One of the most important aspects of reason, which has many ways of expressing itself, is that of conceptual, argumentative, demonstrative reason. It fulfils an essential and irreplaceable function owing to the fact that the kind of knowledge philosophy searches for is a perfect kind of knowledge capable of reaching truth and knowing when it knows in a stable manner, sheltered from subterfuges and surprises. But we are not yet in the sphere of wisdom, rather in that of the episteme (*scientia*). Argumentative reason is capable of lifting itself above the empirical phenomena and the contingency of the cosmos to arrive at some kind of knowledge of God who remains an object which cannot be circumscribed by any human knowledge.[19] For such an outcome one does not necessarily need an intrinsically religious philosophy. An autonomous philosophy, such as the one of Aristotle, will necessarily reach philosophical theology. Therefore the positions of scepticism which are 'speculatively negative' and find it impossible to enunciate anything on the absolute, are rejected. Consequently reason does not possess only a purely critical capacity aiming at the denunciation of the negativity of the existent. As a counterpoint theme in defence of speculative reason, we find in the pontifical document the idea of a *contemporary crisis or eclipse of reason*, not merely its increasing separation from Revelation. Reason seems bent on its own destruction as an organ suitable for the understanding of ontology, morality, politics and aesthetics.

Nevertheless speculative reason and philosophy are only a part of that complex life of the spirit which constitutes a mansion with many rooms. In an effort to encompass the whole intentional life of the human spirit we will meet as sisters art, poetry, music and literature. In these formidable productions of man we will be surprised to meet in the most unexpected forms a divination of the spiritual within the sensible which shines through the beautiful. There we find the expression of a feeling and a nostalgia for something that transcends the merely human level and on which Baudelaire has written in his commentary on Poe: 'It is this admirable, immortal instinct for the Beautiful which allows us to consider the Earth and its spectacles as an essay, a correspondence of Heaven. With the mediation of and through poetry, with the mediation of and through music the soul intuits the splendours which are beyond the tomb.' Dostoyevsky's dictum according to which beauty will save the world may not be completely true.[20] Philosophy, however, knows that one of the most significant names for God, perhaps the most secret and surrounded by mystery, is 'Beautiful'. Plato's *Symposium* can be read as an itinerary of ascent towards the contemplation of beauty.[21] In metaphysical contemplation the beautiful is acknowledged as the radiance and the splendour of all the transcendentals put together (being, unity, truth, goodness). Unless we want to limit ourselves within the important but partial section of a knowledge that cannot be disputed, we have to acknowledge that reason and faith can communicate on the question of truth, since philosophy aims at the beautiful as the highest and most hidden face of being, and faith too aims at God, supreme beauty.

In the relationship between faith and reason beauty enters surreptitiously as an uninvited but not unwelcome guest and surprises us; on the one hand, it mediates a name for God; on the other hand, with its fragility, the fragility proper to beautiful things, it reminds us of death and the beyond, something that the *Zeitgeist* would like to eliminate from the mind's gaze. So that reason does not shun those aspects of philosophy, it is necessary that we think not only according to a utilitarian, scientific, instrumental, agnostic model, but rather within a sapiential horizon and a type of knowledge which can be characterized as tasty, luminous, synthetic. We adopt the word 'sapiential' because we would like to pause here over the fact that the Italian word for wisdom is 'sapienza', that for knowledge is 'sapere', and the root of both those words is the same as that of the adjectives 'saporoso' (tasty) and 'sapido' (palatable). From their very origin wisdom and philosophy proceed in tandem, since the guiding goal of philosophy is ultimately the search for wisdom. He who searches is on a journey and knows that he has not yet arrived. Only the slightly foolish ambition of absolute rationalism can delude itself with its ability to reach wisdom and to transform itself in absolute knowledge, infinitely sure of itself, where philosophy removes its name of seeker and pilgrim of wisdom.

Be that as it may, this temptation is by now behind us; if anything the opposite prevails nowadays. Within contemporary culture the element of wisdom is a precarious condition; at the root of this sad condition there could be the loss within philosophy, and even within theology, of the theme of wisdom with the corollary crisis of Christian wisdom as an edifice which within its differentiated unity incorporates, in ascending order, *philosophical* and *theological* wisdoms, that of the saints or of the *Holy Spirit*.[22] We should note that, whereas the first two are wisdom of knowledge and may be built within the elaboration of the concept, the third kind is a wisdom of knowledge and love which lead to higher transcendent regions and ultimately towards mystical experience.[23] It would be useful to survey (but this is beyond the limits of this essay) the fundamental stages by which, under the banner of a growing split between faith and reason, there has developed a crisis of the intellectual contruction of a Christian wisdom within which even philosophy (especially metaphysics) was understood as wisdom: humble but necessary. In fact, the long and fruitful relationship between theological and philosophical wisdoms constitutes a specific treasure of Christianity.[24] An even more radical and integral element of Christianity is the idea of *Sophia*/Wisdom as eternal divine fullness, with the corollary issue of the implications of such a conception, where to the tortuous human search complies from a distance a transcendent fullness.

In the issue of wisdom we discern the overcoming of the fragmentation of knowledge and of the crisis of meaning in order to reach a unitary vision of what is known. There is an invitation here not to remain complacent within the 'culture of the fragment', adept perhaps at drawing detailed maps of this or that place of the human spirit but unable to go further; an invitation which implies a deep understanding of contemporary thought. The growth of such a culture, which leads to a confusing proliferation of analytical knowledge at the expense of speculative sapiential knowledge, runs the risk of admitting the victory of the instrumental reason, with the resulting difficulty on the part of the subject to establish some order and priorities within himself so that it can govern himself. This situation has been around for a while now and one would not need much imagination to comprehend how much work will be needed to resolve it. Hegel had already observed that the Enlightenment is care of the 'regional'. If it is true that we have lost the patrimony of the intellectual unity of a whole civilization, its recuperation will not happen by simply travelling along the two opposite paths of 'only faith' or 'only reason'.

Philosophy of Being

If we consider it important to stress the great relevancy of the *philosophy of being*, it is because from such a philosophy could emerge a unifying energy capable of going beyond the analytical and the fragmentary. Such a doctrine has been built as an explicit knowledge in a long intellectual journey which begins with the ancient Greeks and is still going on. Within that journey the great Christian thinkers are the ones that contribute to the deepening of this kind of knowledge. Their philosophy can be identified as a philosophy of being because there is a consistent and resurgent effort to know existence, to discover the origins and relations of things. Among the greatest of these stands out Thomas Aquinas, with his doctrine of the act of being (*actus essendi*). Within *Fides et Ratio* we find some powerful expressions on the philosophy of being, something that dogmatic and moral theology cannot do without:

> If the *intellectus fidei* wishes to integrate all the wealth of theological tradition, it must turn to the philosophy of being, [which] is a dynamic philosophy that views reality in its ontological, causal and communicative structures. It finds its strength and its perennial validity in the fact that it is founded on the very act of being which allows for a full and global opening towards the whole of reality. (n.97)

Without this cognitive anchoring the natural light of the mind will not be able to discover another just as powerful, thus beginning to be unsure of itself and turning towards the fragment.[25]

As a consequence contemporary philosophy, which has by and large dismissed the philosophy of being, has rendered itself impotent to establish speculative statements on the whole. The whole remains without garrison, unprotected by science which, while being very powerful in many fields, remains powerless in dealing with the whole; and unprotected by philosophy itself, given the fact that many schools of thought have reduced it to mere psychological, spiritual, literary or narrative expression. The thought of the last decades, when it was not concerned only with praxis and has taken a look at the issue of being, has travelled a descending parabola with its own internal coherence. In the first place it has passed from being as *eternal* to being as *future* and as *coming* (within an all-encompassing concept of revolution, the Marxist but later the Nietzschean also), and later to being as *poverty* and *decline*. It has gone from an ontology without adjectives to an eschatological ontology, and finally to a weak and frayed ontology mirroring a subject who is intimately discouraged about the possibility of finding any meaning and is satisfied as well as it can with whatever it happens to find in the field. At the same time the deposition of knowledge, strictly tied to that of ontology, has proceeded *pari passu*, rejecting the episteme as a mere chimera and replacing it with a future interpreted as progressive, or in decline, depending on the vagaries of culture.

As we can intuit, this dislocation is pregnant with consequences at the level of the articulation and the meaning of fundamental philosophical concepts. There is plenty to choose from. The gamut runs from the idea that it is no longer possible to apply to God the concept of being, to the mantra, so often repeated as to come close to chatter, that the whole of metaphysics has failed in distinguishing the ontological difference between entity (*ens*) and being (*esse*); to the issue (also of Heideggerian provenance) that being has been understood as identical to being present; all the way to the judgment according to which metaphysics renders inconceivable human history as well as the possibility of the new and of freedom itself. Regarding the last issue we could here mention Felice Balbo, a metaphysician passionate about the concept of being, and for whom the metaphysics of being as *actus essendi* makes it possible to think of a future as different from the mere repetition of the present. Moreover the antinomy between metaphysics and change as thought out by Ernst Bloch, and resolved by adopting a concept of being that is conjugated only in the future tense, is an unfortunate equivocation that until recently had various followers. For indeed there are no theoretical impediments why metaphysics should in principle be against change.

All these tendencies and others of a similar nature were catalogued 25 years ago by Bontadini under the concept of 'dehellenization',[26] by which he meant the rejection by a considerable part of Western philosophy of the Greek heritage, particularly the ontological one. This characterization seems appropriate as long as one does not fail to mention that not applying to God the concept of being is more properly equivalent to a 'debiblicization' rather than a 'dehellenization'. God as being is revealed to us by the Bible rather than by Hellenism, where He is described as the Unmovable Mover (Aristotle) or the One (Plotinus), not as the biblical '*Ego sum qui sum*'. *Fides et Ratio*, by expressing a favourable option for the philosophy of being, does not 'dehellenize' and neither does it 'debiblicize'. Even though the biblical concept of God is not a photocopy of the Greek concept, they are alike in at least one essential aspect: the affirmation of God as original perfection.

Once this idea of God is abandoned, we will arrive at a different conception of existence, conjugated in the future and revolving around the humanistic commitment to the world.

The recalling of metaphysics and especially that of being is a counter-point to what is a rather recent phenomenon occurring within the perimeter of Catholicism and analogous to what characterizes almost all contemporary culture: the abandonment of metaphysics and of the very issue of truth. Besides the intellectual fragmentation that this entails, one can observe consequences even within theology; it too seems at times to be less attentive to the question of truth. Together with all these dislocations, to which others within the culture could be added, we notice a diminishment in philosophy and in the life of faith of the importance of 'arguing and giving evidence' (*logon didonai*), submitting the reasons why we adopt a specific solution. In philosophy this is due to a weakening of primary intellectual perceptions and of the argumentative process. Within the life of faith it is due to the primacy attributed to witnessing and to experience at the risk of forgetting the apostle's injunction: 'always ready to answer those who inquire about the reason for the hope that is in you' (*First Epistle of Peter* 3, 15s). Consequently we have come to understand Christianity only as an experience, forgetting that it is also a knowledge and a wisdom. Within this narrowing of horizons, more or less intentional, there is at play a limited and problematic idea of knowledge understood as mere technical functional competence: a functional knowledge to be used for practical ends (best exemplified by the word 'skill'), which in present-day schooling and culture seems to be the only paradigm for the concept of knowledge, a paradigm that undervalues its basic sapiential aspect.

Within the conceptual space which gives priority to the philosophy of being, we could group together other noteworthy points. First, there is the higher rank of revelative or theoretical reason, compared to technical instrumental reason. On this subject we find in *Fides et Ratio* an affinity with the severe criticism of instrumental reason by the Frankfurt school, which had intuited that the demise of revelative reason would eventually open up an abyss: 'The death of speculative reason, which was at first the handmaid of religion and later its enemy, may turn out to be catastrophic for reason itself.'[27] By extending Horkheimer's thought we seem to have arrived at a perspective which deserves a long meditation: with the crisis of speculative reason, while we arrive at the apex of (theoretical) nihilism, appears the difficulty which ensues for man when he attempts to understand a possible Revelation. As to the listening of Revelation, nihilism is an event because of which, once the wellsprings of the contemplative intellect have dried up and the mind has been transformed into instrumental reason, what comes out of the mouth of God can no longer be understood in its own sense. Nihilism is like a sterilizing agent that makes the mind impotent to refer to objects in a contemplative mode and therefore it becomes unable 'to see' and 'to hear'. With the eclipse of the phanic–revelatory character of being, which is no longer grasped by the intellect, the revelatory character of the Word is tarnished. When everything is understood with categories of utility and of 'being at hand' for all possible transformations, so that strictly speaking there is no longer anything to unveil, then the very idea of a divine Revelation enters into a crisis.

Second, by presenting the philosophy of being as the summit of philosophical thinking, *Fides et Ratio* seems to suggest between the lines the perspective of a 'third navigation', that is, that after the Platonic–Hellenic 'second navigation' there has occurred within philosophy a progression, a going forward which is incarnated in the philosophy of being with the conceptions of being as *actus essendi* and of God as *ipsum esse per se subsistens*. This is in line with the idea that Revelation, by challenging the mind, stimulates philosophical thinking to undertake a new journey, a new 'navigation' so to speak, which leads it to a more penetrating contact with the truth of being. In this idea of a 'third navigation' we meet an important aspect of the cooperation between philosophy and Revelation, which is a hinge of believing thought: philosophy goes forward towards a progressive encounter with truth, thus obtaining a better understanding of itself and its purpose. While staying within its borders, philosophical thinking, stimulated by a superior energy, is not a walking of paths leading nowhere.

Third, in any case, the importance attributed to the philosophy of being does not seem to lie so much in apologetics as in speculative motives: solidity, adequacy to the real, shunning of forgetfulness of being, and capacity to think about the whole. Yet the legitimacy of other philosophical orientations compatible with Christianity is never denied. The *Seinsphilosophie* is a proposal, not an imposition. It is preferred because it is considered the most adequate for theological, dogmatic, moral tasks. In fact, the modern and contemporary Christian authors which are eulogized at n.74 of *Fides et Ratio* cannot all be placed within the category of the philosophy of being. They are mentioned because they have successfully held together philosophy and theology, reason and faith. In n.59 it is recognized that the renewal of Christian culture was not due only to Thomism or neothomism, but also to other schools, among which those who, beginning with an analysis of immanence, opened up the journey towards the transcendent (perhaps an implicit reference to Blondel?), as well as those which adopted the phenomenological method.

Finally, there is the passage from the psychological emphasis on the subject to a different kind of anthropology in order to individuate as a task for the thought of the future the development of an ontologic anthropology, based on a methodology that is consonant with the characterization of man as 'he who searches for Truth'. Since truth is relative to being, to say that it is characteristic of the human to search for truth comes close to asserting that the dignity of man is rooted in his relationship to being. By moving from emphasis on the subject-centrism to a form of ontocentrism one can understand *man ontologically*, rather than *ontology anthropologically*. Then the ontology is not a human science because it focuses not on man but on being, although, as any other science, it is elaborated by man.

Biblical Metaphysics

The metaphysical instance as a place wherein there is at least a partial revelation of being and the fundamental structure of everything there is can be articulated with the biblical text within a hermeneutical circle which proves fruitful for both: metaphysical reason helps us to grasp the ontological affirmations which are present in the Bible. On the other hand, the Bible is an inexhaustible source of inspiration for believing thought, so that we can call the product of this hermeneutical circle 'biblical metaphysics' or even 'Christian metaphysics'.

In a preliminary way we can also observe that the recourse to metaphysics can extend to the right understanding of the Bible, in which we find numerous ontological affirmations for whose understanding a phenomenic or a relativist philosophy would be inadequate. Within Revelation, understood as God's word to man, there is a transmission, through various literary means, of a core truth on being, on God, on man and on the cosmos and their destiny; we find there a metaphysical structure which is not compatible with just any philosophy. To exemplify briefly, we will find in the very first verses of the Bible an entire metaphysics according to which God and the world are infinitely different: the world is not God, nor his necessary emanation, and neither is it of divine essence. Nor is it uncreated and self-generating; that is, it is not the Absolute. It is contingent and changing, called into existence from a free act of the Absolute. This excludes any kind of pantheism or a self-sufficiency bent on excluding from the finite any reference to the infinite. We can derive similar considerations from an anthropology tied to those few initial verses, beginning with the idea of man as *imago Dei*, a person and a free being. In several of his works, Tresmontant has demonstrated the existence of a 'Christian metaphysics' present within the Scriptures and Christian dogmatics. Their perspectives include an ontology, a doctrine of the world, of matter, of historical becoming, of action, which are all different from those of Greek thought: 'Christianity carries a metaphysical structure that is not that of *any* metaphysics; it is original ... face to face with the metaphysics of India, Greece, and of modern Non-Christian or semi-Christian Europe.'[28]

To the repertoire of biblical metaphysics belongs moreover the negation of materialism and, on the anthropological level, the delicate issue of the soul which tormented ancient thought and which is resolved by conceiving the soul as neither existing from eternity (*ab aeterno*), nor uncreated, nor divine, nor migrating, but created as immortal. Within this concept we can identify the doctrines of the first few lines of the *Credo* which form, in an extensive sense, what we could name the 'metaphysics of the *Credo*'. When we recite the sequence: 'Credo in unum Deum Patrem omnipotentem, factorem coeli et terrae, visibilium omnium et invisibilium', we see declared there the unity of God and his omnipotence, thus refuting the thesis of the existence of two supreme principles; that is, the theosophic–gnostic position according to which God has created only souls and invisible realities, while visible material realities are the work of an evil demiurge.

By considering the historically undeniable fertilization and stimulation that the Bible has exercised on philosophical thought, it is worth noting the introduction in the philosophical realm of concepts which belong to philosophy by their very nature (whose task it is to clarify them), but which remained outside its scope before the arrival of Christianity: concepts such as creation, personhood, a richer notion of nature, the notion of God as being (perhaps already faintly intuited by Aristotle – cf. *Metaphysics*, 1073a, 23), the real distinction between essence and existence in all created beings and their identity in God,[29] and in the moral realm the concepts of evil and sin, the non-existence of a first principle of evil, and so on. Pre-Christian philosophical tradition did not perhaps completely ignore these notions, but remained more or less in darkness and in a perplexed uncertainty concerning them. It is due to the works of Christian thought that philosophy has taken hold of those truths with a firmer certitude and has then explored them more fully. Revelation is not for philosophy an external limitation or a negative norm, but an inspiration and a stimulus that reaches and fertilizes the sources of the intellect. Without that inspiration the intellect will not attend to some very important problems. A significant proof of this is the forgetfulness by some contemporary philosophies of the problem of evil and pain which is central to the biblical horizon.

A positive outcome is better assured when believing thought remains faithful to an important rule, that of the vital intercommunication, the continuity and the reciprocal support among the *habitus* so that the superior ones support the inferior. Which is to say that the theological *habitus* and evangelical contemplation spiritualize and render more powerful the metaphysical *habitus*. The encyclical *Aeternis Patris* (1879) with its ancient form confirms this norm: 'Far from diminishing or extinguishing the vigour of intelligence, the added light of faith perfects it, and increasing its strength makes it suitable for higher things than those to which it is naturally predisposed.' Therefore 'Christian philosophy' remains philosophy, something that, while belonging to this world, is put in a better condition: it is the kind of philosophy which reaches maturity, journeying inasmuch as it can towards the knowledge of the truth of being.

As Gilson has repeatedly observed, the existence of Christian philosophy within a mediaeval context is predicated on the fact that Augustine is not simply repeating Plato, that Aquinas or Duns Scotus are not a mere Aristotle badly understood, which means that such a philosophy possesses its own originality and its own thematic field. That purported immense vacuum between Plotinus and Descartes, a sterile philosophical desert of almost fifteen centuries as even sustained by E. Bréhier in his *Histoire de la philosophie*, is an assertion worthy of a fairy tale (for Bréhier there is no trace of philosophy in the Fathers of the Church, in Augustine, in the entire Middle Ages, but merely a juxtaposition of heterogeneous elements, a mixing-up of dogmatic assertions with philosophical propositions devoid of any rational value). However, Gilson's conclusion in his *The Spirit of Medieval Philosophy*, one of his most successful works, is that the Judaeo-Christian Revelation can be considered a religious source of philosophical development;

Latin Middle Ages are testimony to such a development. One may counteract this conclusion by maintaining that what has been influenced by a religious faith has ceased to have philosophical value; this, however, is a rationalistic postulate contrary to reason. A philosophy that is inspired by revelation is not ipso facto a false philosophy; it will be true if it happens to be a good philosophy. In fact the Latin Averroists, who deliberately withheld their philosophy from any influence of Christianity, gave proof of philosophical sterility. A philosophical thought which is free from what Vico calls 'the arrogance of the learned' is better able to encounter man and to grasp all the richness, complexity and chiaroscuro of existence.

Notes

1   The great esteem of *Fides et Ratio* towards philosophy confirms the same warm esteem expressed in the encyclical *Aeterni Patris* of Leo XIII (1879), according to which it is upon philosophy, 'a most noble discipline among disciplines', that 'to a great extent depends the correct orientation of all other sciences'. This particular underscoring of the importance of philosophy for believing thought is an ancient position which finds its valid confirmation in scholasticism, especially in the works of Aquinas, who put the question thus: 'utrum sit necessarium, praeter philosophicas disciplinas, aliam doctrinam haberi' (whether it is necessary to have, in addition to philosophical disciplines, a different doctrine) (*S. Th.*, I, q. 1, a. 1).

2   Jean Danielou, among others, confirms that the road of reason only, or of faith only, cannot be taken by a believing thought that wants to remain in equilibrium without sacrificing anything: 'If rationalism, the pride of a spirit that dares to take possession of God in order to dispose of him, constitutes a great danger, so much the more it is worthy of admiration the courageous effort of intelligence that while respecting mystery does not give up understanding, that goes to the limits of its possibilities and only stops when it encounters a light so bright that it blinds. This courage of intelligence in exploring mystery remains the great legacy of Saint Thomas Aquinas. It is a difficult equilibrium only rarely achieved within the parallel abysses of rationalism and of fideism' ('Le Dieu des philosophes', in *Dieu et nous*, Paris: Grasset, 1956, p.59).

3   Schelling's philosophy has reflected on the element of wonder: 'It is a well known statement of Plato that the passion of the philosopher (*to pathos tou philosophou*) is a wonder in itself (*to thaumazein*). If this statement is true and profound, then philosophy, rather than being limited to what must be understood as necessary, will feel the urge to go beyond what it regards as necessary, and which does not provoke any wonder, to what is outside and above and beyond any necessary examination of knowledge. It will find no rest till it has arrived at something that is worthy of absolute wonder' (*Filosofia della rivelazione*, edited by A. Bausola, Bologna: Zanichelli, 1972, vol. II, p.121).

4   Cf. *Phaedo*, 67 a ff 'Those who philosophize correctly exercise themselves in dying ... and for them death is much less frightening than for other men' (67e). On a bad philosophy that wants to do away with the reality of death, see also F. Rosenzweig, *La stella della redenzione*, Genoa: Marietti, 1985: 'The reality of death which cannot be eliminated from this world ... transforms in a lie, before it can even be thought out, the fundamental thought of philosophy, the idea of a unique and universal knowledge of Everything' (p.5).

5   We hear at times that it is necessary to do without the very notion of truth as conformity in order to emphasize the notion of meaning where supposedly the metaphysical tradition is lacking. But upon reflection one realizes that the concept of truth is

originative, while that of meaning perhaps is not. Meaning may refer to the meaning of
a sentence, or to the truth content of truths. In the first case, if we ask, 'What sense has
sentence A?', we are asking about its intelligible content, if for instance its subject and
predicate concord or contradict each other, without raising the problem of its veracity
vis-à-vis the real. In the second case the notion of meaning, even if used in all its power
and not as the mere sum of fragmented truths, echoes the notion of truth.

6   *Critica della ragion pura*, "Logica trascendentale", Rome–Bari: Laterza, 1983, p.98.
7   Ibid.
8   *Il fondamento della conoscenza*, Brescia: La Scuola, p.23.
9   Cf. ibid., p.27.
10 *Al di là del benee de male*, Milan: Adelphi 1988, I, 4.
11 E. Kant, letter to Hertz, 21 February 1772 (It. trans., *Epistolario filosofico 1761–1800*,
    Genoa: Il Melangolo, 1990, pp.64–75). Regarding the reasons for idealism ultimately
    being unable to solve adequately Kant's problem, I suggest the considerations of *Terza
    navigazione. Nichilismo e metafisica*, (Rome: Armando, 1998), where the issue is
    discussed vis-à-vis the neo-idealism of Giovanni Gentile.
12 For this aspect, see for example the essay of J. Haldane on realism, in which he
    dialogues with H. Putnam: 'On Coming Home to (Metaphysical) Realism', *Philoso-
    phy*, 71, 1996, pp.287–96.
13 Cf. M. Dummett, *Le basi logiche della metafisica*, Bologna: Il Mulino, 1997, and
    W.V.O. Quine, *Il problema del significato*, Rome: Ubaldini, 1966.
14 This study is included in the volume of K.O. Apel, *Discorso, verita, responsabilità*,
    Milan: Guerini, 1997, pp.65–168.
15 Ibid., p.72.
16 Cf. *Being and Time*, n.44. This striking Heideggerian formula appears to carry some
    equivocations concerning the very nature of truth. I will not pause here on this aspect,
    which is diagnosed in *Terza navigazione: Nichilismo e metafisica*, pp. 176–81.
17 H. Jonas, 'Mutamento e stabilità', in AA.VV., *Su Heidegger. Cinque voci ebraiche*, ed.
    F. Volpi, Rome: Donzelli, 1998, p.92.
18 Perhaps in the *Qohelet* we can recognize, as in a filigree, a negative or apophatic sort
    of theology which claims to know almost nothing about God and his ways. This
    theology has deep roots in many cultures and finds its most powerful expressions in
    Taoism. From *Daodejing*, the book of Origins (*dao*) and of its virtue I transcribe the
    following sentence: 'The *dao* which can be named *dao* is not the eternal *dao*. If its
    name can be pronounced, it is not its eternal name. That which is without name is the
    beginning of heaven and earth. The measurement of man is the earth, the measure-
    ment of the earth is heaven, the measurement of heaven is the *dao*, the measurement
    of the *dao* is itself.'
19 The roads to God have been and are still being contested in various ways, depending on
    the era and its cultural style. One of the most insidious contestations claims with
    Nietzsche that 'everything that is demonstrable is of little value'. However, with the
    five ways of Aquinas (and let us not forget the sixth of Maritain) God is known as the
    unknown; He is not demonstrable or subject to our ways of measuring. Aquinas with
    his usual profundity writes on the subject: 'Dicendum est quod, ex quo intellectus
    noster divinam substantiam non adaequat, hoc ipsum quod est Dei substantia remanet
    nostrum intellectum excedens: et ita a nobis ignoratur' (*De potentia*, q. 7, a. 5, ad 14m).
    On the power of theoretical rationality expressed by the five ways of Aquinas, 'relevant
    today more than ever', cf. John Paul II, *On the Threshold of Hope*.
20 Regarding this matter, cf. Dostoyevsky's *The Idiot*, where the nihilist Ippolit asks
    prince Myskin: 'Is it true, prince, that once you said that the world will be saved by
    beauty?' and then adds, 'Which beauty will save the world?' (*The Idiot*, PtIII, ch.5).
    This is a pertinent question since there are at least two great forms of beauty: an
    aesthetic one perceivable with the senses, and a transcendental kind graspable with the
    intellect and expressing the face of being. The first kind, which borders on the sensible
    and the intelligible, carries something great and fragile as intuited by Dmitrij Karamazov
    ('The frightening thing is that beauty is not only terrible, but it is also a mystery').

21 'He who has been led to this point by the doctrines of love, contemplating beautiful objects systematically and correctly, he, having arrived at the end of the discipline of love, will detect – in an instant – something beautiful and admirable in his own nature ... something that is eternal, that is, that is not born nor does it die, that does not replenish itself nor is diminished and that is not part beautiful, part ugly ... Think now of what would happen to somebody who was able to see beauty itself, pure, without stain, unmixed ... divine beauty in all its simplicity' (210e).

22 'There is no doubt that, for a long time now, our culture has been dominated by the spirit of science which looks for the knowledge of created things, and secures the unity of its vision by its own Promethean thrust' (AA.VV., *Sagesse*, Bruges: DDB, 1951, p.9.

23 'We are not saying that Christian wisdom is nothing but philosophy: it goes beyond philosophy just as grace goes beyond man ... The recourse to theological wisdom, which journeys bathed in the light of faith guided by reason and resolves, by revealed doctrines, the perplexities of human experience, will constitute one of the indispensable stages in the installing of evengelical behaviour, for which our era thirsts, perhaps without even knowing it. However, what constitutes the internal connection and the ultimate blossoming of Christian wisdom is the infused wisdom of the saints which is supernatural even in its *démarche*' (ibid., pp.10, 17).

24 With the emphasis given to the veritative–contemplative moment, we perceive in all its ambiguity the idea – defended by Heidegger – that the knowledge emanating from faith within the circuit of *fides quaerens intellectum* is not true knowledge but a simple positive element. For the German thinker, '*theology is a positive science and therefore as such is to be distinguished from philosophy in an absolute manner*' ('Phenomenology and Theology', in *Segnavia*, Milan: Adelphi, 1987, p.7; original emphasis).

25 'The Thomistic notion of *esse* (being) is the last one by definition. It is the last Thule of every metaphysics, the foundation of a metaphysics valid for all times' (E. Gilson, *Le philosophe et la théologie*, Paris: Fayard, 1960, p.255).

26 Cf. G. Bontadini, *Metafisica e deellenizzazione*, Milan: Vita e Pensiero, 1975.

27 M. Horkheimer, *Eclisse della ragione*, Turin: Einaudi, 1977, p.23.

28 C. Tresmontant, *Les idées maîtresses de la métaphysique chrétienne*, Paris: Ed. du Seuil, 1967, p.11 s. Cf. also, by the same author, *Etudes de métaphysique biblique*, Paris : Gabalda, 1955, and my essay 'Il Concilio Vaticano II e la filosofia cristiana', *Doctor Communis*, XXXV, 1980, pp.31–50.

29 This discovery issues from the Bible, not from Aristotle or the Greeks, as Aquinas warns us: 'In God essence is identifiable with existence. Moses was given this sublime truth from God when to the question "If the children of Israel should ask me what your name is? What should I answer?", the Lord said, "I am who I am"' (*Ego sum qui sum*) (*Contra Gentiles*, l. I, c.22).

The text of Exodus 3:14 has been established as central for the Christian theology of a patristic and scholastic kind beginning with Augustine, through Anselm, Aquinas, Bonaventure and so on. Some exegetes assure us that the text has not been well interpreted, that its sense is another, which begs the question: 'Has Christian theology deceived itself for almost 2000 years?' An unbiased reading of the Exodus passage seems to confirm that, Moses having asked God for his name, He reveals it to be 'I am.' With this answer God is not teaching metaphysics or a concept of being; he leaves it up to the philosophers to discover that within his words.

When, in his *Itinerarium mentis in Deum*, Bonaventure (Ch. V) deals with 'de speculatione divinae unitatis per ejus nomen primarium, quod est *esse*', he is refuting *ante litteram* the too famous Heideggerian assertion on ontotheology which understands God as *ens supremum*, that is, as the apex of a chain of beings. And if the witness of Christian theologians were not enough, one could refer to that of Avicenna, who observes that *Primus quidditatem non habet*: since God does not have an essence, He is exactly at the opposite pole of any being (*ens*) which is such because it encompasses a quiddity. As per Gilson, this statement of Avicenna characterizes the highest point ever reached by natural theology (cf. *Costanti filosofiche dell'essere*, Milan: Massimo, 1993, p.200).

Chapter 2

Interval on Modern Thought

The Separation of Reason and Faith

The Church's interest in philosophy, which has increased in the last century and a half, as is testified by two Vatican Councils and the encyclical *Aeterni Patris*, is an event deserving of some reflection since, where philosophy is concerned, we have seen the most intense and long-lasting confrontation between modernity and the Church: within this confrontation have happened the most striking dialectics, the greatest quarrels and the greatest difficulties which, going beyond theory, have put on flesh and blood and have entered historical reality.The idea that modern history is really a 'philosophical history' is not without validity, in the sense that it has issued in some part from philosophers' minds. Beginning especially with the Enlightenment and the French Revolution, the dissensions, already potentially present in the 16th and 17th centuries, flared up, reaching their culmination in the 19th century and part of the 20th century. Even today, the Church's judgment on modern philosophy, while being more subtle and varied, more serene and without the anathemas of the past, does not hide persisting reservations.

If we look at how *Fides et Ratio* conceives of modern thought, we notice in the first place that the Church does not embrace the idea that there has been a homogeneous development of philosophy, claiming rather that within modernity has occurred an important caesura which was introduced by the so called '*novatores*'.The outline of the history of philosophy developed in the encyclical reveals that, contrary to the powerful Hegelian reconstruction, the historical succession of metaphysical systems is not the logical development of the fundamental determinations of the Idea. Hegel wrote in this regard: 'In the activity of thinking spirit there is an essential continuity, and one proceeds rationally. We must approach history, particularly the history of philosophy, with this trust in the world spirit.'[1] Rather, what we discover within the history of philosophical thinking are as many gains as losses, ascensions and tortuous paths in which lurk the best and the worst.

There are passages in *Fides et Ratio* where credit is granted to modern philosophy for some positive aspects and great merits: for example, the development of the attention given to man, to history and to the problem of knowledge, the care for the universe of knowledge, the contemporary development concerning logic, epistemology, philosophy of language, philosophy of nature and the existential approach to the analysis of freedom. Perhaps not by chance this enumeration does not include metaphysics, ontology or ethics: the disciplines which have been the traditional core of philosophizing where – it seems implicit – there have not been great developments, and in fact there may have occurred some regressions. Nor is it by chance that in talking about ancient philosophy the word 'masters' is used, a title not accorded to modern thinkers. This leads one to believe that in the opinion of the encyclical the shadow elements, dubious or even negative judgments are prevalent as far as modern philosophy is concerned, to the point that one has to ask whether part of modern thinking is fit to favour that *fides quaerens intellectum*, that search for a genuine self-knowledge of faith, which constitutes a hinge of Christian thinking and a norm of its theology, or rather whether it does not succumb to agnosticism, relativism and scepticism. A common horizon of the diagnosis, often mentioned, is a radical mistrust of reason's ability to know and the end of metaphysics, at which late modern philosophy has arrived. This descending dialectic had favoured the *essor* of instrumental reason for goals of social utility and power.[2]

The separation between reason and faith, philosophy and theology is individuated as that spiritual experience which rarely has allowed within the modern fruitful relationship between philosophy and the word of God: 'the legitimate distinction between the two forms of learning became more and more a fateful separation' (n.45). This separation was individuated as a negative element even in *Aeterni Patris*, which declares that 'the best philosophers are those who join the study of philosophy to the respect due to Christian faith'. That harmony between reason and faith which had been reached by patristic and mediaeval thought was compromised by those philosophies which predicated rational knowledge as separate and as an alternative to faith, often reaching explicit dualism and even contraposition which methodically ignored truths derived from the light of God's message to man. This movement began in the 17th and 18th centuries and reached its zenith in the 19th century with idealism, atheistic humanism and positivism, and with the transformation of revelative reason into instrumental reason. All these aspects can be said to coalesce, leading to the loss of the sapiential dimension of philosophy in its search for meaning. The positions to which the critique of the encyclical refer can be traced back to a kind of anti-realism which denies the ontological objective knowledge, preferring to indulge in phenomenism, relativism and the refusal of metaphysics without which it is pure illusion to gain access to the sphere of the transcendent. They can also be traced back to the principle of immanence, not yet overcome, which mediates the pretension of an absolute self-foundation of reason within the insuperable circle of self-consciousness.

At the end of this negative dialectic we discover the most disturbing phenomenon: nihilism as a 'consequence of the crisis of rationalism' (n.46). With this reference to nihilism enters upon the stage a key concept of modern philosophy, a concept intensely debated in the last 150 years, but absent up to now from explicit teaching of the Church. Perhaps the Vatican I Council happened rather too early for it to pronounce itself on the matter. That was not the case for Vatican II which, however, remained silent on it. This issue of nihilism appears late in important documents of the Church, but when it finally does it is in a forceful and effective mode (we will treat this in Chapter 3). The so-called 'weak' postmodern, which has proclaimed that the times of certitudes are over and finished with the arrival of those of the absence of any meaning, is not immune from nihilism to which the encyclical attributes an unequivocally negative meaning, rejecting those currents which conceive of it as something positive.

The factors we have enumerated, although they are showing a moderate Christian influence on modern philosophy, have not substantially changed within contemporary thought where *Fides et Ratio* individuates some critical points: eclecticism, historicism, scientism, pragmatism and nihilism. It is worth stressing here that scientism and historicism echo the two great powers of modernity: science and history. In varied measure, to these can be traced some positions which nowadays enjoy great favour, even if not shared by all. We will mention two: (a) the thesis, of Heideggerian origin, of the end of metaphysics and of the coming of a post-metaphysical thought, and (b) the orientation towards a universal fallibility according to which it is impossible to reach any kind of stable knowledge about anything, with the corollary thesis that the only legitimate cognitive activity is that of criticism, never that of a positive construction.

This historical picture would be lopsided were we not to integrate within it those philosophers and modern theologians capable of articulating faith and reason together. They were not modern as regards the speculative matrix when it manifested unmotivated enmity towards Revelation and raised the idea of a 'separate philosophy', but they were modern on a personal level: they lived, operated and fought within modernity, critically examining its premises and reformulating them when it proved necessary. The papal document eulogizes the work of numerous modern Christian thinkers who have worked for a dialogue between Revelation and reason: Newman, Rosmini, Maritain, Gilson, Stein. Significantly the list includes names from Eastern Europe – Soloviev, Florenskij, Caadev, Losskij – with an opportune valorization of the *orientale lumen* and of the work of Soloviev, which is named first (cf. n.74). In this nomenclature we have one of the most innovative tracts of the encyclical which integrates and renews a tradition which sometimes was in danger of being ritually repeated, where the patristic period was surveyed, then the mediaeval, coming to a stop with the 13th century (this basic outline is still noticeable in *Aeterni Patris*). *Fides et Ratio* has a different approach, suggesting the idea that philosophy of a metaphysical kind and open to faith is a living reality within a great traditions (one of the greatest traditions of human culture of all times), not an event to be relegated to the remote past. Perhaps some would have liked to see added to this list other contemporary names, for example, those of Blondel, Guardini and Marcel. However, what is not cited is not necessarily excluded, as we gather from n.74: 'other names could be cited'.

It does not take much prophetic talent to predict that the rather brief mention in the encyclical of philosophical modernity will give rise to debates and objections. The philosopher and the historian of philosophy could raise some objection to the judgment there expressed, thus assuming the very horizon in which the encyclical situated itself, the modalities of the relationship between faith and reason. In fact, some important thinkers of the era of Humanism and of the Renaissance, of the 17th century are bypassed; for those the judgment that they 'placed rational knowledge on a separate course and as an alternative to faith' is a rather misplaced definition. One thinks of Nicholas of Cusa and, especially, Ficino who in the 15th century attempted to head off the rift between *pietas* and *sapientia*, and between religion and philosophy by searching for a synthesis between Christianity and Platonism. For the later era one thinks of Malebranche, Vico and, up to a point, Leibniz. While Descartes considers the separation between faith and reason acceptable, that is not the case for Malebranche and Vico. Malebranche attempted a synthesis, convinced as he was that their collaboration was to their mutual advantage, contrary to the antinomy that Pascal's apologetic places between them. Now, it may be true that these thinkers did not enjoy an intellectual influence comparable to those that are criticized; their mention, however, would have attenuated somewhat a complete but not very believable vacuum that supposedly existed between the 13th century and the first half of the 19th century when, with Newmann, Rosmini, the neoscholastic revival, and then the encyclical *Aeterni Patris*, we have a rebirth of a philosophy that does not separate faith from reason. That would have provided with more concreteness the diagnosis of *Fides et Ratio*, which observes that 'a good part [therefore not the whole] of modern philosophy has been moving further and further away from Christian Revelation'. Moreover, a moment of autocriticism is missing in the reconstruction of the modern relationships between philosophy and theology; that is, the acknowledgment of the responsibilities located in the Church's life. The alienation of philosophical schools from Revelation and the scanty conditions of Christian thought (one thinks especially of the 18th century) are phenomena which are internal, not only external to the Church.

Despite some interpretative limitations, due in part to the methodological canon utilized in analysing modernity (the relationship between faith and reason), *Fides et Ratio* establishes a continuity with the Vatican II Council. In fact, the cultural dynamics and the interpretation of the Council have developed in separate ways: there are positions which in certain postconciliar currents have been attributed to the Council but which it did not intend to affirm. And there are others that it did proclaim, and sometimes repeated with insistence, which have been ignored following the problematic assumption that it did not say them and that in fact it did not want to support them. The relevancy of philosophical thinking for evangelization and the possibility of reaching a knowledge of the meta-empiric belong to those things that the Council did say, although several later acted as if it had been silent about them.[3] Contrary to what obtained in the past, the danger now is not that of an excessive trust in reason, which at one time intended to do away with Revelation, but that of an inadequate trust in a reason which now believes that its proper place is that of trafficking with the sensible as a stockbroker of the finite. While many voices admonish thinking not to search for things that are too high, Revelation invites it never to stop in its search because it can rest only in the Absolute, and this it can do only if it stops declaring itself self-sufficient. The whole of philosophy 'needs to be completed because, in the last resort, all that is finite is, inasmuch as it is created, placed in relation to God, and that is not exhausted with the resources proper to philosophy'.[4]

These reminders bring us back to the long philosophical contention, which has been going on for two centuries especially in Europe, but not only there, between those who proclaimed immanentist, atheistic, secular philosophies on the one side, and Catholic thought on the other side. This extraordinary debate, in which one of the highest manifestations of the human spirit and a supreme moment of philosophical research were realized, deserves to be remembered as something great and should be saved from oblivion. One way to achieve this purpose is to explore what some notable exponents of Catholic philosophy (some of whom were among the best modern philosophers, including Maritain and Rosmini, to name but two) thought of modernity. I would like to review their judgments, focusing on a small but significant group of French and Italian thinkers of the 19th and 20th centuries. With some surprise, one arrives at the conclusion that the fundamental paradigm of analysis and methodology which they developed towards modernity is close to the one of *Fides et Ratio* (as well as to that of the earlier *Aeterni Patris*). Within the critical dialogue of Catholicism with modernity it is hard to discern what exactly was the contribution of the Church's magisterium and what that of Catholic philosophers in the articulation of an interpretative model. On the whole it appears homogeneous, which seems to point to a considerable reciprocal influence.

Modern Philosophy in the Judgment of Catholic Thought

To begin the investigation, and that is all we will be able to do here, we propose to review the main trends of the interpretation of modern philosophy as drafted by certain Christian thinkers in the 19th and 20th centuries. We will refer to Gioberti, Rosmini, Maritain, Fabro, Del Noce, Balbo and Leo XIII, whom Gilson considered the greatest of Christian philosophers of the 19th century. The reader should not expect here a systematic development of the theme but merely broad probings which may however turn out to be as significant as more elaborate analyses. Leo XIII is the promulgator of the encyclical *Aeterni Patris* which, despite the fact that it was written 120 years ago, is the most immediate progenitor of *Fides et Ratio*, which welcomes past judgments in its chiaroscuro evaluation of the modern age.

There are several common points of view between the two encyclicals. Even a cursory glance will yield the following: the increasing separation of philosophy and faith, beginning in the 16th century; the reclaiming of philosophy's task in discovering truth, not excluding the truth about God; the importance of the recourse to philosophy by theology; and the increase of power that the light of faith brings to intelligence. Despite the lapse of time and the spiritual transformation that have since occurred, the adversaries of both documents remain roughly a rationalism closed within itself and a fideistic irrationalism. This basic continuity, although with different modulations and bifurcations, should not be too surprising to those who know the care with which the Roman ecclesiastical magisterium assumes, assimilates and elaborates its past positions.

In the first half of the 19th century, Catholic theology and philosophy reacted to modern currents (sensism, positivism, immanentist or atheistic rationalism) – all movements that radically question the rational and metaphysical foundations of human knowledge. At first this happens by recourse to traditionalism at times allied to ontologism. According to traditionalism, man does not receive the truths that are relevant to his life from his own reason, but rather from the great and long-lasting river of tradition. Opposing the anti-traditionalism of Descartes, traditionalism considers human intelligence an imperfect, or at least subordinate, tool of investigation. Within it we find a constant criticism of reason which is understood as a mere connective and discursive faculty without any intuitive and metaphysical capacity unless stimulated by the encounter with God's word; unless, that is, it accepts Revelation through faith and authority. Perhaps without realizing it, traditionalism makes its own Kant's criticism of metaphysics. In such a traditionalism, treating with great suspicion anything that issued from the French Revolution (considered the mother of every deviation), we see delineated a remarkable anti-modern attitude both on the philosophical and on the civil level.

Although Leo XIII was personally hostile to ontologism and traditionalism as specific philosophical schools, the tone of *Aeterni Patris* – even if substantially oriented to replace condemnation with invitations to restore Christian philosophy – is not without similarities to the doctrines of traditionalism of a De Bonald, or a De Maistre, or of the first Lamennais, or Bautain (the importance of tradition and the criticism to the *novatores*). The complaint of the traditionalist school towards Thomism and more generally toward scholasticism was that they constituted a deviation from authentic Christian philosophy. The authors of traditionalism, contrary to Aristotelianism, were impregnated with French spiritualism, partly of classical Cartesian derivation, and especially with Catholic romanticism. However, towards the middle of the 19th century they began to distance themselves from Lamennais while orienting themselves toward Aquinas. The encyclical of Leo XIII, by opposing both the current of Christian rationalism and irrationalism, elects the cause of peace between faith and reason which, albeit distinct from one another, should lead to a philosophy coordinated and united with faith. What remains strong, however, is the anti-modern dimension which in part transfused itself into the speculative Thomism of the 20th century, albeit in a more positive vein: less focused on the errors of modernity than on the ability of Thomism and of Christian philosophy to renew itself and walk towards the future.[5]

A common trait of Christian thought of the 19th century is the diffidence towards the *novatores* of the 16th century (*novatores saeculi sexti decimi*, one reads in *Aeterni Patris*) and the strict connection established between the world's evils and the 'pernicious' doctrines which have issued from the philosophers' schools: it is widely held that the first cause of a civilization's decline is intellectual, and consists in the disorder of the mind. The main responsibility of the *novatores* was that of starting to philosophize after having separated themselves from faith's content and thus distancing themselves from the past philosophical tradition. All of a sudden the innovators set aside faith and theology, as well as metaphysics, venturing out on a new journey defined by Gioberti as 'psychologism' and by Bontadini a century later as 'gnoseologism'. This was a step pregnant with many consequences, given the fact that for the Christian thinkers we have mentioned the fundamental process of reality is ontological, not gnoseological or psychological. Turning now to Gioberti, we see that he never tired of asserting that the substance of philosophy is in ontological and theological science: 'A false kind of philosophy, after a long circuit of errors, did away with the idea of God from human knowledge. A true philosophy has as its task that of searching for a scientific God, to pacify through knowledge the spirits with religion, and may be defined as the instauration of the idea of the divine within science.'[6] In this diagnosis we find a basic agreement in the 19th century and in part of the 20th century with an approach approved by *Aeterni Patris*.

When Gioberti tried to identify the profile of philosophical modernity he individuated Descartes (and indirectly Luther) as the principal corruptor of philosophy in modernity: Descartes begins philosophical psychologism (which today we would perhaps call 'subjectivism'), Luther begins religious psychologism. We are dealing with two reformers, as Maritain sees them 80 years later. The methodical fault which is present at the beginning affects modern theology and philosophy. According to Gioberti, starting with Descartes, the French derived all the most negative consequences, attenuated in the Germans by a residual influence of Christian doctrine. They too, however, arrived with Kant, who follows Descartes, at the absorbing, in the *Critique of Pure Reason*, of ontology into psychology. Gioberti interprets Kantism as nothing but Cartesianism taken to its logical conclusion, and to a certain extent as the scholastic rearrangement of Descartes, while English philosophy remained more tied to common sense. Within French philosophy sensible perception dominates, while in German philosophy ideal or intellectual intuition is privileged, leading sooner or later to pantheism, wherein Gioberti saw the greatest surrender of German philosophy.

On the assumption that 'the Idea remains splendid and pure in the hands of the magisterium ... and there anybody who wants to philosophize successfully may find it',[7] Gioberti agreed with the censorship decree issued by the Congregation on the Index against Descartes' philosophy (20 November 1663). He recognized within modernity a little group of isolated philosophers who remained orthodox and a succession of heterodox thinkers who broke with tradition. Their main faults were separation from tradition and separation from religion. Although Gioberti does not confuse philosophy with religion, he holds that 'philosophy is not possible unless founded by and presided by religion' (p.35). For him the core of ontology was to be found above all in religion to which was to be added speculation, so that the same truths which were axiomatic at the level of religion, were then treated anew as theorems in philosophy. Hence, in contrast to Descartes and the psychologists, philosophy is not assumed to be a science in itself separate from theological dogma. Perhaps it was due to this alliance, which Gioberti thought that some philosophers had preserved, that he considered Leibniz, Malebranche and Vico the truly great modern philosophers, the only ones who were comparable to the ancients: 'I am absolutely convinced that authentic philosophy, in its substance not just its antecedents, has ended in Europe with Leibniz and Malebranche' (p.36). As regards Vico, he says that 'this great genius has few equals in the history of speculative sciences' (p.118).

From his youth, Rosmini pursued the idea of a restoration of philosophy after the devastation wrought on it by the authors of sensism and subjectivism, 'a medley of negations and ignorance which under the assumption of being philosophy invaded the whole of Europe with greater damage done to true knowledge than any barbaric invasion ever did'.[8] Regarding the constant confrontation with modern philosophical thought, which one finds in almost every one of his works, we will limit ourselves here to only one element, his critique of rationalism (be it philosophic or theological) which cuts to the root any possible cooperation between philosophy and theology by considering reason not only autonomous but perfectly self-sufficient, and grounded on itself. It is well known that the fight against rationalism was one of the greatest battle fronts of Christian thought in the 19th century. In his study, whose title is translated as *Rationalism's attempt to penetrate theological schools*, Rosmini considers rationalism a principle which in a nutshell comes down to this proposition: 'Man must admit nothing but what is suggested to him by natural reason to the exclusion of any supernatural illumination.'[9] Therefore this constitutes the heresy of 'our century'. Rationalism 'ignores any enlightenment from on high, abolishes any supernatural order, and reduces man to his natural state only', so that man ends up trusting only natural reason, refusing any help from Revelation and grace, assuming as its guiding principle a reason separated from Revelation. Rationalism cannot be understood only in its logical–gnoseological sense as an excess of trust in the veritative and argumentative ability of human reason; rather one must include in its understanding, in a full existential sense, its refusal of the supernatural as a closing of man upon himself and as a rejection of Revelation's assistance. This Rosminian understanding of rationalism is perhaps the greatest confrontation that we find in *Fides et Ratio*. It looks upon rationalism as an attitude which places faith in permanent danger.

Rosmini identifies at the very root of the process leading to a full-blown rationalism the refusal of the dogma of original sin, without which redemption is useless and the main motive for the Incarnation is demolished. Within rationalism there is the desire to free man from any dependence, including that on God, who at times seems to assume the identity of a boss; in any case, it conceives of Him as far away, absent from the world and its concerns. To a certain extent it is a world without God whose obverse is a God without world. The separation between civil life and the Church is nothing but the corollary of the distance between God and the world which can sustain itself in its adult worldliness and according to its own principles.

In Maritain's writings we find a constant thematization of modern philosophy running from his first works until the last. He is just as far from the Enlightenment and the idealistic paradigm of modern philosophy seen as a process of continual ascension towards a better and higher truth, and reaching its zenith with the Hegelian paradigm,[10] as he is from the reactionary's paradigm of the 19th century (De Bonald, Donoso Cortés, De Maistre), which is often nothing but the turning upside-down of the other, as it understands philosophical modernity as a process towards the plenitude of error. Already in *Antimodern* (1922) Maritain is not to be found under such a flag, despite the fact that his judgment on the metaphysical and gnoseological foundations of modernity is non-compromising. The difference between his and the pure anti-modern position is constituted by the idea that indeed it is possible to have progress in philosophy and therefore the philosophy of being has a constructive task in the matter. In prefacing *Antimodern* he observed that 'What I call *antimodern* could just as well be called *ultramodern*. It is well known that Catholicism is as much antimodern as regards its attachment to tradition as it is ultramodern as regards its courage in adapting to new conditions emerging from the world's life.'[11] The reference to tradition appears with a positive connotation, to the point that the innovating philosophers of modernity, because of their demonstrated disparagement of the thought of preceding generations, are considered intellectual barbarians.

Well then, if 'modern philosophy is full of treasures that it would be absurd to neglect them, it can teach us some very useful things' (p.94); and besides, it would be naive to neglect its two constitutive elements which Maritains individuates as the principles of *immanence* and of *transcendentality*, within a by now taken-for-granted separation of faith and reason. The first criterion (immanence) is understood by Maritain as a sort of reclaiming of the self's independence, of the internal in relation to the external; a kind of forgetfulness of what is other, so that 'every act, every help, every norm, every teaching that derives from the other (from the object or from authority, be it human or divine) is seen as an attack against the human spirit'. The principle of transcendentality incorporates the idea that there are no data by which we can be measured 'since nature and laws, definitions, dogmas, duties are nothing but pure expressions of our inner subjectivity and of the creative activity of the spirit in us' (p.12). The two principles are therefore understood as a manifestation of the absolute independence of the creature who proceeds – so to speak – *etsi Deus non daretur* (as if God did not exist).

Approximately 45 years later the issue of modern philosophy is taken up once again in Maritain's *Le Paysan de la Garonne* (The Peasant of the Garonne) through the polarity realism–idealism, and arriving at conclusions that are not too dissimilar from those of *Antimodern*. The speculative ascension of his diagnosis revolves around the issue of otherness and of being, which according to Maritain is sacrificed by those who begin with thinking:

> I refer to Descartes, the father of modern Idealism and all his successors who, while performing changes to his system, on the whole followed an evolutionary curve of an irresistible logic. They all begin with thinking and they stop there, whether they deny the reality of the things and of the world ... or whether in one way or another they reabsorb them within thought.... They deny at the outset exactly that from which thought originates and without which it becomes a dream – the reality to be known and to be understood, which *exists*, is seen, is touched, is grasped by the senses ... the reality about which and beginning from it a philosopher worthy of the name will question himself and without which he is nothing. They deny the absolutely first foundation of philosophical knowledge and research.[12]

Here we see that this beginning with thinking only, that is, idealism, becomes anti-realism, one and the same as forgetfulness of being, rejection of otherness, not excluding the otherness represented by Revelation and towards which faith tends.

Felice Balbo (1913–64), who died prematurely, has left us an opus which, while not being very vast, is intense in its power, despite some youthful immaturity. In Italy he was one of the few secular thinkers who discovered and then appropriated the philosophy of being by a personal and intricate journey of research, ranging from a dissatisfaction with idealism (especially that of Gentile) to a warming up to Marxism (for a while he understood Marx as the Galileo of social sciences), which led him to Aquinas and the philosophy of being originally understood by him as a conquest of 'man without myths'. Since his death interest in his work within Italian culture has been rather scarce and desultory, but there is a remnant of interest in his thought as evidenced by some publications about him.

Balbo's particular evaluation of modern philosophy was expressed in sharp, at times pitiless, judgments which, while needing more development and the support of critical–historical articulations, nevertheless carry a farsighted lucidity. We will limit ourselves to quoting the author; but we wish to draw attention to the fact that these quotations have the characteristic of a personal conquest as well as homogeneity with the diagnosis we are developing here. A very keen judgment of Balbo, almost a declaration of the death of modern philosophy, sounds thus: 'Modern philosophy in its entirety has failed historically and the whole of philosophy as explicitly expressed until now must be, in something essential, either mistaken or inadequate, or both.'[13] While modern philosophy is so depicted, Balbo considers contemporary philosophy essentially a philosophy of crisis (remember that the example before him was that of existentialism), which he considers authentic because it refuses any prop to cover up the situation while remaining unable to suggest a positive way out of the predicament.

Besides the philosophy of crisis he individuates the new possibility offered to contemporary thought in an historically renewed recovery of speculative philosophy 'in the sense of a development historically new and metaphysically homogeneous of the Aristotelian–Thomistic line ... It is in fact the only philosophy that does not succumb to the criticism, even merely theoretical, of the Marxist praxis (as on the contrary has happened to rationalism and particularly to Hegel in their essential theoretical profile), inasmuch as it does not want to "theologize" the becoming, but to know being' (p.251). What in his youth Balbo defines as Aristotelian–Thomistic philosophy, according to the paradigms then current, he will later call 'philosophy of being'. He will invariably assign primacy to this philosophy for a variety of reasons. We recall two of them: (a) its radical realistic stance which unites the primacy of being and the beginning from the a posteriori, and (b) the fact that it carries a concept which is unique and extraordinarily rich in the history of philosophy, that of being as act of existence (*actus essendi*) which is possibility, growth, intensification and dynamic perfecting for the finite entity. Balbo interprets the doctrine of *actus essendi* in a totally different sense from the Parmenedian image of being as a full, immobile sphere closed upon itself.[14]

We should add that for Balbo, as well as for Maritain, an anti-modern theoretical position does not automatically imply an anti-modern position in the civil–political realm, in fact it includes the possibility of an ultramodern twist.[15]

Within the evaluation of modernity by C. Fabro (1911–95), especially expressed in his *Introduzione all'ateismo moderno* (Introduction to modern atheism), we find a consideration that is unmistakably critical of the principle of immanence, which, according to the author, is intrinsic to modern philosophical thinking and necessarily leads to atheism. In a cadence which begins with the Cartesian *cogito* and then finds expression in a philosophy closed within the immanence of the act of consciousness, the self becomes unable to escape from the circle of identity with himself and find the other. The modern atheistic mode of thinking has its premise in the Cartesian system with which, according to Fabro, 'incipit tragoedia hominis moderni' (begins the tragedy of modern man). 'Both its supporters and its adversaries are in basic agreement on the interpretation of modern thought; i.e., on the new path taken by thought originating with the principle of immanence: it consists of a turning away from the object towards the subject, from the world to the self ... Even for classical thought knowledge was an immanent process ... and therefore [within it] the knowledge was a perfective process, which does not constitute being. In modern thought, on the contrary, immanence is constitutive and foundational in respect to being',[16] which is to say that consciousness originates from itself. As Fabro sees it, there is within modern thought an 'atheistic core value' which is to be considered not as facultative but as constitutive, in the sense that any concession to transcendence by the same would constitute a misunderstanding and a logical contradiction face to face with the criterion of immanence with which this new beginning operates. It follows that, with these premises, the issue of a final rapprochement between philosophy and Revelation cannot even be postulated, since Revelation constitutes the foremost example of otherness, of difference in respect to the circle of self-knowledge. Hence within philosophies that issue from the *cogito* and that remain closed within it, God's word not only cannot be heard, being outside one's consciousness, but, for the same reason, has to be excluded in its very possibility.

Like Fabro, Del Noce (1910–89) individuates in the problem of atheism the issue which is at the core of philosophic modernity, even if his diagnosis pursues its own peculiar path. While for Fabro atheism connotes *axiologically*, and in a certain sense without residues, modern thought, for Del Noce 'the birth of atheism characterizes modern philosophy only problematically',[17] and therefore it encompasses two directions: 'Besides the direction towards radical immanentism, there is also that towards reconciliation with tradition (from Descartes to Rosmini and beyond, in the direction of the rediscovery of Thomism).'[18] According to Del Noce, the very movement of Gentilian actualism could be understood as an introduction in reverse to a revival of classical metaphysics.

This individuation by Del Noce of a positive path in modernity, from Descartes to Rosmini and touching Pascal, Malebranche and Vico, where atheism is excluded, renders modern thought a non-unitary process with distinct approaches and therefore open to integrations and linkages. With the introduction of a double development the secularist emblem of modernity as a process inevitably directed towards immanence and atheism is placed in jeopardy.[19]

After these overviews, we can gather together in a few paragraphs the perspectives where we can individuate substantial agreements among the Christian thinkers of the 19th and 20th centuries we have mentioned.

First, what comes to the fore, sometimes explicitly and at other times implicitly, is a structural element of the greatest importance: a refusal to separate philosophical logos from Revelation, Judaeo-Christian principle from Greek principle. In several of them the problem is an explicit theme: in Gioberti with his protologic discourse and his respect for ancient philosophy; in Del Noce through his 'Christian Platonism'; in Maritain through the idea of a double election: the natural election of Hellenism and the supernatural election of Christianity. There is a common front erected against a 'dehellenizing' thrust which has been quite strong within theology and Christian philosophy in the last half of the 20th century, under the slogans 'Away from Athens!' or 'Away from Scholasticism', or even 'Away from Aquinas!'

Within a philosophical–theological progressivism, a path has been taken which attempts to pull apart, as much as possible, the Judaeo-Christian principle, which is accepted, from the Greek principle, which is considered completely different from the former. It is felt that in accepting metaphysics Christian thought has been subordinated to Hellenism and therefore biblical thought is betrayed in the process. It is perhaps worth noting here that, in this way, a road was taken that was contrary to that of various gnostic currents eager to absorb Christianity within Hellenism. At this point we understand in a new light the refusal of *Fides et Ratio* to accept any opposition in principle between philosophic logos and revealed logos, an aspect of this opposition being the dehellenization attempt. The authors we have examined held firm to both Athens and Jerusalem, thus avoiding the slogan 'neither Athens nor Jerusalem', so in vogue within European neo-pagan nihilism and so different from the ancient 'Jerusalem yes, Athens no' (or the opposite), which accepted either a biblical exclusivism or a Hellenic one. Rather, they have included within the edifice of Christian philosophy both Athens and Jerusalem, recognizing the necessity of metaphysics but also its humility before the wisdom of the Holy Spirit; that is, ultimately placing Jerusalem above, but not in opposition to, Athens.

The result of this process dealing with the relationship between Christianity and Hellenism has been a Christianization of Hellenism more than a Hellenization of Christianity. The method which presided at their encounter is based on a dialectic of illumination, discernment, assumption and refusal where Christianity was the regulating and directive moment. In fact, we could individuate in this process an original form of completion and transvaluation of Hellenism, in the sense that Hellenism is understood in depth, integrated, corrected and opened to new gains. This method remains a paradigm for every possible communication between Christianity and the culture in which it finds itself; one that could yield positive results if the criterion utilized for the encounter is confirmed: they met each other because Christianity exercised a discernment on Hellenism and because there were common bases between them such as a non-secularized culture, a widespread religiosity, the sense of truth, the aspiration toward the absolute, and so on. To the contrary, with a dehellenized modernism one gets the impression that the regulating criterion of an encounter must be found within the culture of modernity rather than in Christianity. Hence, in the dialogue between Christianity and modern culture, there is a need to abandon the two extreme positions: that of fundamentalism which wants to avoid the dialogue because it would deprive the Gospel of its originality, and that of modernism insisting that modern culture mediate a pre-comprehension and a self-knowledge of the human, which is peculiar and original.[20]

Second, the interpretative paradigm of philosophical modernity proposed by Pope Leo XIII in his *Aeterni Patris* (which of course had preceding elaborations and studies of previous Catholic thinkers) is substantially received and accepted in the framework of *Fides et Ratio*. There we find at least four aspects which are accepted as diagnostic elements and are considered still valid: (a) the turning away, similar to a caesura, which has resulted in the development of philosophy due to the *novatores* between the late mediaeval era and the beginning of modernity; (b) the increasing gap between philosophy and theology; (c) the difficulty of reviving once again a philosophy with a Christian matrix or, as *Aeterni Patris* affirms, a 'Christian philosophy'; (d) owing to the divorce between philosophy and theology it is no longer philosophy but science which decides the destinies of the world, with the danger of philosophy being reduced to an insignificant sideshow. To this essential horizon, *Fides et Ratio* adds a particularly relevant development with reference to the philosophy of being and its corresponding metaphysics, an indispensable theoretical light for a valid philosophy and theology. In this underlining we encounter a homogeneous integration with respect to

Aeterni Patris suggested by the looming question of being in the 20th century and by the correlative endogenous development of the philosophy of being and Thomism. We are therefore presented with possible passage from a speculative anti-modernism to the ultramodern, characterized by the postmodern revival and development of the philosophy of being.

This philosophy presents itself as a positive and active possibility for the future, owing to the fact that the most authoritative versions of modern metaphysics, that is, metaphysics of criticism, those of the mind and of the spirit, have encountered great difficulties and seem to have arrived at a terminal exhaustion. In them what is most arduous is the constitution of a positive nexus between philosophy and theology in the sense of a hermeneutical circularity which remains significant for both, and which is actually practised by the Christian thinkers we have examined. They understood it as capable of restoring vigour and meaning to Christian conceptualization.

Within this methodological framework we can locate some difficulties of post-tridentine theology which, being confined within the ecclesiastical perimeter of seminaries, needs philosophy and must know it in depth in order to function as a hermeneutic of the kerygma and as intellect of faith, arguing in their favour. This is especially true for systematic theology, which reflects upon and analyses the fundamental contents of faith and can develop while acquiring and integrating philosophy within itself. In this respect, in several areas of Western culture, a *conventio ad excludendum* has been adopted, a kind of agreement between the 'theological right' and a 'secularized left' to marginalize theology from the market-place of civil society.

Third, the necessity of not accommodating themselves to the separation of philosophy and theology, reason and faith convinces Christian thinkers to interpret the philosophical thinking of modernity, placing on the table not only metaphysical, gnoseological categories, but also theological ones (such as the nexus between nature and supernatural, freedom and grace). The destination of this journey should be the understanding of the modern speculative event, not a mere apologetic or confessional end. They are convinced, in fact, that at a conceptual and historiographical level it is impossible to understand modern thought without putting it in relation to theological thought, so that the history of philosophy and the history of theology are seen as inseparable. *Le grand siècle* of Europe, and we do not mean just France, would be incomprehensible were we to leave out of consideration the theological preoccupations with which it was concerned and that found expression in Descartes, Leibniz, the Port Royal thinkers, Malebranche, Spinoza, and so on.

Fourth, contrary to Heidegger's judgment, the interpretation of the historical and conceptual development of philosophy from the Greeks all the way to us, as the two encyclicals of Leo XIII and John Paul II reveal, and as is concretely present in the thinkers on being, does not arrive at a judgment of universal decadence. The crisis has to do with the fundamental aspects of modern philosophy and not with the whole of Western post-Socratic philosophy. Which is to say that the neglect of being is not universal diacronically or syncronically; rather, it is 'regional', that is, relative to a precise period and to certain philosophical systems. This means that the journey towards a recovery of a non-'ideosophic' philosophy is possible through a reconnection with existence and a realistic noetic.

Finally, the passage from a 'metaphysical' and contemplative Christianity to a non-metaphysical one is not favoured and judged valid when it is understood in historical Blochian terms as a mere project for freedom and justice in the world and aiming at the future of the world. The eventual outcome of such a project is a resolution–dissolution of Christianity within politics due to an endogenous secularization. This can have two possible outcomes: an exclusive emphasis on the Bible, assuming as paradigm its political use and its incompatibility in principle with metaphysics, or a subordination of Christian culture to secular thought patterns.

A Short Digression about Contemporary Thinkers

Our attention has been intentionally directed toward philosophers belonging not to present days but mainly to past times, though not too far in the past. We may now ask why *Fides et ratio* does not refer in its argumentation to present-day thinkers, be they believers or non-believers. The fact that they are still living is not perhaps a fundamental negative reason, although this aspect could have some importance in the ecclesiastical style.

Arguably there are deeper reasons for this silence. In trying to interpret it, we start from a basic question, formulated as follows: to what extent can contemporary philosophy be helpful to Revelation? A thought which in its expression by the most internationally known names (for less celebrated thinkers, the situation could be different) either has removed the relation between philosophy and Revelation – mainly on the ground of an agnostic and sometimes atheistic assumption – or has adopted in philosophy an unrestricted fallibilism and a correlative scepticism, can hardly be helpful. These authors express positions different from that sustained in the papal Letter. As the Revelation is an autocommunication of God to man, by its very nature it is divine word expressed in human language: then it is intrinsic at its presence in the history the renewed trial of going toward a better comprehension of its content. For this task neither any language nor any philosophy is suitable. It would be curious and contradictory to apply to the divine word an atheistic thinking or a completely agnostic philosophy.

Some examples can be gathered from the present, very various philosophical landscape. Habermas' thought has for almost two decades expressed a firm and, up to now, unrevoked choice in favour of fallibilism and of post-metaphysical thought (see *Il pensiero postmetafisico*, 1991; *Faktizität und Geltung*, 1992). Ranging himself under the flag of historicism, Habermas maintains that theology, when cooperating and merging with metaphysics, is only an outmoded form of the spirit (see *Texte und Contexte*, 1991). Rather surprising is the 'aporia' between a firm fallibilism and the assumption that post-metaphysical thought saves and protects an unconditional meaning without having recourse to God. In the positions of K.O. Apel, we meet a refined version of the idea that truth is grounded on an intersubjective consensus in the ideal community of communication. Parting from Popper, who maintains fallibilism and the doctrine of truth as conformity in the meaning of realism, Apel asserts that fallibilism must be freed by this doctrine and connected to a theory of truth as consensus and convergence in the unlimited community of researchers (see the article, 'Fallibilismo, teoria della verità come consenso e fondazione ultima' in his book, *Discorso, verità, responsabilità*, Milan, 1997). Rorty posits the end of philosophy and of argumentation, as for him philosophy is a literary genus which does not differ in itself from any other expression, such as tale and narration. Nominalist and anti-realist thinkers deem it necessary to refuse the idea of truth as conformity and to reduce it to an attribute of a few propositions.

Coming to agree with Dewey on naturalism, Quine has firmly affirmed that his philosophy is naturalistic and that there is no first philosophy: 'With Dewey I maintain that knowledge, mind and meaning ... must be studied with the same empirical spirit which fosters the natural science. There is no room for a "first philosophy"' (see *Ontological Relativity and Other Essays*, 1969). In *Word and Object* he maintains that the very idea of physical object is a myth and can be used only as a useful postulate, an assumption which leads to the epistemological holism. This and the dissolution of the object entail the crisis of philosophy as an enterprise capable of autonomous knowledge. In Dewey's pragmatism what is remarkable is the doctrine on the instrumental and operating character of ideas and theories, considered as utility functions for the active arranging of a determined environment. If this happens, ideas and theories will be true (see *Renewing Philosophy*, 1919). The pragmatistic notion of truth suggests that the measure of the truth of ideas is their capability of success and effective operation (in this assumption it seems that the notion of truth is based on that of moral and political action).

It would be unfair to question the considerable talents and contributions of the above authors. If even, it is the general characteristic of their asking which raises doubts, as it does not deal with the principles and the general structure of reality, which encompasses also the problem of the infinite. For in their questioning lacks radicalism, it is unlikely that a thought limited within the experience and the temporality can be suitable in arousing problems on the relation between finite and infinite.

The great majority of these authors, with some minor exceptions, do not consider the relation reason–Revelation in their works. Paying a tribute to the principle of immanence, which sometimes is stronger for being less declared, they assume as indisputed a deep secularization of philosophy, which usually means that it is reduced to ethics, while it cannot involve itself with metaphysics and Revelation. Compared to the past, the difference is striking, as in times of rationalism it was a reason very sure of itself which expelled as fairy tale faith and Revelation; now it is a reason limited and uncertain to express a preference for the finite. In my opinion those philosophers reveal inadequacies on the level of the philosophical research, for they adopt reductionist views at the very beginning; their thought is subject to the oblivion of being, as its question is omitted; they do not show enough consideration of the speculative wealth of the tradition they reject. A highly problematic role is played by the rather rude form in which theory of knowledge (gnoseology) finds itself in their works. As theoretical philosophy as such is dismissed and replaced by science, the realm of philosophy limits itself to the reflection on scientific knowledge (epistemology) and mainly to ethics. Consequently, when a look is directed towards Christianity, they will consider in it mainly or only the moral aspect.

These scanty considerations could explain why *Fides et ratio* is silent in respect of present-day philosophers: their reason does not seem open to the trascendent. This situation has been detrimental to faith and reason: 'each without the other is impoverished and enfeebled' (n.48).

Notes

1 G.W.F. Hegel, *Lezioni di storia della filosofia*, Florence: La Nuova Italia, 1973, vol. I, p.29.
2 In the evaluation of philosophical modernity we notice parallel points between the encyclical's web and the argumentation by John Paul II in *On the Threshold of Hope*, where one finds, for example, the passage within modernity from metaphysics to the philosophy of knowledge.
3 In continuity with Catholic tradition and the teaching of the Vatican Council I, Vatican II has affirmed that human reason is not limited by the horizon of the empirical: 'Intelligence is not restricted to the sphere of phenomena, for it can arrive at intelligible reality with true certitude, even if, because of sin, it remains partly obfuscated' (*Gaudium et spes*, n.15); 'The Sacred Synod professes that "God, origin of everything that exists, can be known with certitude by the natural light of human reason from created things"' (*Dei Verbum*, n.6).
4 Edith Stein, letter to Jacques Maritain, 16 April 1936, in *Cahiers Jacques Maritain*, n.25, December 1992, p.38.
5 To understand the importance that Leo XIII conferred on *Aeterni Patris*, it would be enough to note the words he proffered in his conversation with the Dominican father Pègues on 1 August 1900: 'Among all my encyclicals the one that is dearest to me and that gave me the greatest consolation is the encyclical *Aeterni Patris* on the restoration of Scholastic and Thomistic philosophy' (cf. *Revue thomiste*, May 1901, p.132).
6 V. Gioberti, *Introduzione allo studio della filosofia*, Milan: Fratelli Bocca, 1939, p.61.
7 Ibid., p.58.
8 *Introduzione alla filosofia*, Rome: Anonima Romana Editoriale, 1934, p.19. In this work there are numerous and well articulated critical judgments on modern philosophy, especially French and German philosophy. What deserves particular notice is the branding of Hegel as a nihilist: 'Things that are not actually considered by thought are *nothing* to thought ... Here we have again the origin of Hegelian nihilism ... The thinker as such does not recognize as existing that which is still not an object of his thought, and consequently he declares it *Nothing*' (p.110).
9 *Il razionalismo che tenta insinuarsinelle scuole teologiche*, ed. R. Bessero Belti, Padua: Cedam, 1967, p.1.
10 'The whole of the history of philosophy is a consequent and necessary progress, rational in itself and determined a priori from its own idea; thus this is the example that the history of philosophy offers ... The last one, the most modern and the newest

philosophy is the most developed, the richest, the deepest' (Hegel, *Introduzione alla storia della filosofia*, Bari: Laterza, 1925, p.57, 62).

11 *Antimoderno*, Rome: Logos, 1979, p.12.

12 *Il contadino della Garonna*, Brescia: Morcelliana, 1969, p.152 f.

13 F. Balbo, *Opere 1945–1964*, Turin: Boringhieri, 1966, p.385.

14 Cf. ibid., p.645.

15 What is particularly interesting in Balbo's writings is his criticism of rationalism, understood as a system which considers being deductible from thought, so that being does not transcend conceived being and logical being includes perfectly the real one. From another point of view, rationalism is that position of thought which assumes the pure and simple identity of thought with its formula.

16 *Introduzione all'ateismo moderno*, Rome: Studium, 1969, p.1010.

17 Cf. *Il problema dell'ateismo*, Bologna: Il Mulino, 1990, p.16. It is worth mentioning that for Del Noce rationalism has various facets, the most striking one being the refusal without any proofs of the supernatural: rationalism excludes what goes beyond the circle of immanence.

18 'The rediscovery of Thomism in Etienne Gilson and its present meaning', in AA. VV., *Studi filosofici in onore di Gustavo Bontadini*, Milan: Vita e Pensiero, 1975, vol. II, p.470. A deeper analysis of Balbo's and Del Noce's thought can be found in my *Cattolicesimo e modernità*, Milan: Ares, 1996.

19 As we have hinted, in Maritain we encounter a reading which does not coincide with those of Fabro and Del Noce. He has in common with Fabro the assumption of the fundamental character of the *cogito* and of the metaphysical–gnoseological moment. He has in common with Del Noce the idea that modern philosophy can hardly be understood as a univocal process towards atheism. The diagnosis of modernity is developed touching various keynotes: from the metaphysical where a primacy of idea and logic over ontology is diagnosed, to the one of realism where the criticism of 'ideosophia' is applied to the principal modern thinkers, to the one where theological categories such as theocentrism and anthropocentrism (one is reminded here of the analysis developed in *True Humanism*), and the relationship between freedom and grace, are placed on the table. We should add that Gilson understood modern philosophical thought as characterized by elements of anti-realism and essentialism, in the sense that the first and immediate object of knowledge is considered essence rather than existence.

In this survey a place should be attributed to the position of the group which worked in preparing the inauguration of the Catholic University of Milan, and where Gemelli's personality stands out. We should mention here two elements which are symptomatic of his positions: a programmatic article of Gemelli significantly titled 'Medievalism' published in the journal *Vita e Pensiero* (1914), and the editorial which inaugurated in 1909 the first number of the *Rivista di filosofia neoscolastica*.

The article (which can be found in *Vita e Pensiero 1914–1964*, Milan: Vita e Pensiero, 1966, pp.11–38) shows clearly a rejection of and a hostility towards modern culture 'so poor in content, so shining in false jewels which are all exterior', so that 'so called modern culture can be identified as the fiercest enemy of Christianity' (pp.11, 15). Consequently, the agenda of the new journal will be 'medieval in substance, very modern in form' (p.21). As to the editorial of the *RFNS*, in conformity with a widely debated issue in modern philosophy, it assigns pride of place to the criteriologic and epistemological problems (the objectivity of knowledge, the problem of certitude), with the aim of recuperating the severely compromised value of objectivity and certitude: 'It is universally known that modern philosophy, from its beginnings, has shaken the unconditional trust in the objectivity of the spirit, of the world ...' (p.6).

Within the metaphysical school of the Catholic University we can consider significant the individuals who establish a dialectical examination of modern thought: Olgiati, Vanni Rovighi, Masnovo, Bontadini, just to mention the best known and the most authoritative names. Worthy of notice is Bontadini's essay, 'The metaphysical deviations at the beginning of modern philosophy' (which became part of *Metafisica e deellenizzazione*, pp.35–53), where the thesis is proposed that modern philosophy by retreating within itself reopens the road to metaphysics 'as science of being as being; since being is now in the position of intentional object of the act of knowing', no longer external and extrinsic to it (p.38).

20 The dialogue between Hellenism and Christianity, which still lives in Catholic thought, was precarious during the Renaissance and the Reformation. The Renaissance opted for the humanistic element; the Reformation chose the Christian element and denounced what the Renaissance recognized in Greek pagan classicism, its humanism. Both separated metaphysics and Christianity even if on different paths: the former privileging philosophy, the latter faith. Consequently it turned out difficult to reach a stable synthesis of the two elements so that many crises of European culture are interpretable at their very root as crises of the relationship of its two souls: comprehension of the human and comprehension of the divine.

Chapter 3

Religion and Biblical Tradition

The Enigma of Nihilism

Upon meeting the issue of nihilism, the reader may raise his eyebrows. The issue is so popular that every tyro writer wants to offer his opinion on it. On that we can easily agree, but the horizon begins to change when we ask what level of elucidation the issue has reached so far. Almost half a century ago, when it was already well known and even 'old', Jünger opined that there still did not exist a clear definition of nihilism: 'A good definition of nihilism ought to be compared to the identification of the cause of cancer. It would not imply a cure but certainly the premise for its cure, in as much as men contribute to it. It is in fact a process that occupies much of human history.'[1] Even today, when the term 'nihilism' has been used in every sense imaginable, as a mark of condemnation and even of approval, there is little to reassure us that the issue is not in a state of utter confusion. Among the many and repeated attempts to arrive at an adequate insight on the essence of nihilism, several remain marginal on the theoretical level since they start out with different and less radical goals. On the other hand, others have done a lot of travelling on this road (I am thinking here especially of Dostoyevsky and Nietzsche). Still others, such as Heidegger, have perceived the strict correlation between nihilism and the oblivion of being, but without being able to articulate in a coherent way how nihilism can be overcome. This is due to the ambiguities that afflict Heidegger's diagnosis of the oblivion of being.

The above may sound rather harsh, but it is not foolhardy. Which is to say that, in order for philosophy to arrive at an adequate definition of the concept of nihilism, it should first arrive at a level of self-knowledge and a meditative power which seem to have been rather scarce in the last few decades. A preliminary observation is that nihilism cannot be a conception by which the whole of existence is reduced to nothingness. Even if some philosophers and literati have not refused this extreme option, it does not constitute any kind of initial progress on the issue, if by nothingness one understands, and it would be legitimate, the *nihil absolutum*. The total annihilation of everything there is, besides being completely beyond philosophy's power, cannot even be posited as a concept from which anything can be deduced: it is a journey wherein thought flounders and the mind, beginning from a pseudo-radicalism, ends up with dimming itself.

On the other hand, the word 'nothing' could be taken as a metaphor for something else: the estrangement from the finite, a sort of abyss, a different name for the totally Other. These are legitimate uses of the term within which, owing to the analogical and metaphorical character of its use, one cannot nevertheless arrive at an adequate definition of the idea of nihilism. Getting to that definition is a debt whose payment cannot be deferred any longer when coming face-to-face with a notable and even epochal event: a kind of nihilism which is subtle, sometimes concealed and impalpable, seems to be the nocturnal tempting angel of Western liberal societies. We should note here that predictions on the duration of nihilism and a possible way out of it are risky. In any case, it is not up to the philosopher to make predictions on what may or may not happen. All he can do is to clear the ground of an idolatrous cult of destiny, and in our particular case perform a separation from the Heideggerian assumption that nihilism is something which is largely independent from human freedom, because it is located within the very history of being which gives itself and hides itself at the same time.

Christian thought, distracted by an age-old confrontation with modern cultures of action, especially Marxism, has been remiss in taking a hard look at nihilism. It has come to it rather late. It has perceived its challenge, it has feared it within the moral plane, has attempted to exorcize it by keeping it at a distance. Rarely has it looked steadily in its eyes. The documents of the Church's teaching (social encyclicals, pastoral letters) have largely and for a long time accused consumerism but almost never nihilism. But now, looking deeper, we are becoming aware that nihilism is an important cause of consumerism and its related hedonism. This leads to an important shifting of perspective from the centrality of consumerism to that of nihilism considered now as a much more radical and disturbing phenomenon.

Fides et Ratio meets this accumulated delay on the issue by offering a definition of nihilism ('What is nihilism?'), a definition which world philosophy has been searching for assiduously, without much success, over the last 150 years or more.[2] To understand this event we must grasp, in the encyclical pithy phrasing, the way in which it presents, as a golden coin in a treasure box, the essence of nihilism. We should add here that the major exponents of Christian thought of the 20th century have in part laid the foundations for a proper understanding of the character of nihilism, without however going far enough, perhaps thinking that the bastion of ethics would have sufficed. As a result of this failure, the dominant philosophical line on the subject of nihilism has been impersonated by other thinkers, especially Nietzsche and Heidegger.

The problem is first approached in n.46:

> As a result of the crisis of rationalism, what has appeared finally is nihilism. As a philosophy of nothingness, it has a certain attraction for people of our time. Its adherents claim that the search is an end in itself, without any hope or possibility of ever attaining the goal of truth. In the nihilist interpretation, life is only no more than an occasion for sensations and experiences where the ephemeral has pride of place. Nihilism is at the root of a widespread mentality which claims that a definitive commitment should no longer be made, because everything is fleeting and provisional.

The encyclical returns to the issue at nn.81, 91 and above all n.90. Mentioning the horizon common to many philosophies which have abandoned the sense of being, the encyclical refers to the nihilistic outlook

> which is at once the denial of all foundations and the negation of all objective truth. Quite apart from the fact that it conflicts with the demands and the contents of the word of God, *nihilism* is denial of the humanity and of the very identity of the human being. It should never be forgotten that the neglect of being inevitably leads to losing touch with objective truth and, consequently, with the very ground of human dignity.

The era of nihilism brings with it the end of certitudes replaced by the absence of meaning.

These two formulations complement each other. The first one, while being clear in grasping the origins of nihilism in rationalism and its crisis, presents some symptomatic features which are not always necessarily tied to nihilism (the reference to the ephemeral); the second seizes on the essential nature of nihilism, especially the theoretical one, which is very often preliminary to and more original than moral nihilism. Four characteristics are put forward: *crisis of the idea of truth, oblivion of being, breakdown of real and objective knowledge and negation of man's humanity*. We might say that (theoretical) nihilism arises whenever the light of the speculative intellect is no longer focused on being, so that men and things are no longer ordered and valued according to their nature and their being.

The original speculative core from which we can trace so many forms of nihilism (first of all theoretical and later, and with specific modes, practical nihilism) can be identified in a compact negative structure – within which some events combine to reinforce each other – in which as many negations are perceptible: (a) a profound existential rift between man and reality, of which gnoseological anti-realism is the most decisive theoretical expression; (b) concealment of being, so that the aim, which was always and continually sought by philosophy, is (no longer) knowledge of being, which it considers obstructed. Eventually that knowledge which is denied to philosophy is replaced by scientific knowledge or by the will to power; (c) victory of nominalism over realism within the framework of a widespread anti-realism, in which generally the concern with being is abandoned for a concern with the text, in the passing from a metaphysical ontology to an 'indirect' ontology of a different kind. The fundamental language of philosophy is no longer seen as that of metaphysics but that of the sciences, or in the hermeneutic axis addressed towards the comprehension of texts and therefore at most within a second degree of immediacy; and (d) an attempt to do without the concept of truth or to transform it by attacking the very idea of truth as correspondence between thought and being. In this compact core of nihilism there also takes place a sort of annihilation or dissolution of the object, considered by some expression of idealism as an unconscious product of the self.[3] As the doctrine which overcomes the opposition between thought and object is anti-nihilistic, within idealism and realism this happens by completely different paths. Realism upholds the intentional identity between intellect and object, as taught by Aristotle, together with the ontic-real primacy of the object (all the light emanates from the object) in the place of the transcendental productivity of the self, which posits the non-self.

Objectively bound up with these fundamental definitions of nihilism, beyond the intentions of the author, is Nietzsche's dazzling statement: 'Nihilism: the end is lacking, the answer to the question "why?" is lacking!' Reality exists, being is a *donnée*, yet everything is without meaning, since it is rigorously impossible to discover any meaning when the ideas of purpose, of intelligibility, of reason of being (*raison d'être*), have failed. Nihilism appears to us here as the loss or the total concealment of meaning, and most probably the refusal of the original, primordial logos as everywhere present in the whole (*en archê ên o Logos; in principio erat Verbum*).[4] If right from the beginning there is logos, this implies that being, life and nature are intelligible, in principle open to the human reason. And reason cannot proceed from an obscure, original abyss of irrationality.

The above-mentioned assumptions, anything but isolated, hold in their grasp, for example, the generative insights that underpin the monumental work of Weber, a lucid yet disenchanted disciple of Nietzsche; for, unlike him, Weber felt no confidence in future philosophy as creation and place of manifestation of the superman (*Übermensch*). The nihilistic character of the work of Weber emerges in many of his formulations. Especially eloquent among them is his statement that culture 'is a finite section of the infinite, meaningless world-becoming, to which is attributed sense and significance from man's point of view'.[5] This formulation confirms that a feature of nihilism is the lack of meaning (the answer to the question 'why?' is missing, the purpose is missing) and its reduction to an act of will on the part of the subject, who to survive and not fall into the absurd posits meaning as a challenge to an existence devoured by becoming and which appears to be hostile, mute, absolutely non-revelatory. The Weberian idea of the modern era as directed by a powerful 'instrumental rationality' is highly dependent on nihilistic presuppositions and mainly on Nietzsche's determination of nihilism as lack of end/purpose. If ends cannot be either known by reason or placed in a hierarchy, then a science of ends will be impossible, and only a science of means – addressed to purposes which will be only decided by desire or by factual power actually in force – is allowed. The 'instrumental rationality' precisely consists in irrationality of ends accompanied by technical decisions about means.

The probings of *Fides et Ratio*, compared with some intuitions of Nietzsche and Heidegger, but transported into a different horizon of thought, help to conceive the post-metaphysical and post-Christian essence of nihilism. It includes a strong 'antinomianism' (*antinomos*), a notable sign of which is the widespread rejection and at times even the hatred of the *lex naturalis*, as well as a comprehension of being and of the cosmos that is no longer revelatory (phanic and theophanic), but mute. Man, engaged in surviving in a hostile cosmos, develops within himself an anti-contemplative spirit and a corresponding inner-worldly activism. If the eclipse of the 'phanic' or revelatory nature of being and an anti-contemplative attitude refer to each other, the search, so common today, for a barrier against nihilism, identified in ethics, risks becoming a diversion. Ethics cannot last long when the realm of truth and meaning is compromised. With clear insight, Nietzsche grasped that the death of ethics would follow upon the 'death of God', if only because (I would add) it is a 'secret agent' in the service of the Almighty.

The nihilistic content of the core in which the rift between man and reality, oblivion of being, anti-realism and the crisis of the idea of truth all come together, is very dense because, owing to its origin, its effects are indefinitely transmitted in many directions. Some of them are the questions of *necessity*, of *essence* and of *substance*, to which the philosophical tradition attributes great importance for the proper understanding of the whole and of existence. It is from the decision not to acknowledge or to erase any dimension of necessity, understanding necessity as that which cannot be different from the way it is, that issues a nihilism which carries to an extreme its will to power and domination, and daring to take dangerous paths; a nihilism that will be eventually defeated, but not before it has done serious damage. Radical versions of scientism seek to do just that: to change the very nature and essence of man. Here nihilism (be it theoretical or practical) reveals itself as oblivion of essences: an oblivion that makes one unaware of the impossibility of changing essences, especially that of man understood as a subsistent individual characterized by intellect or spirit.

I term this attitude *nihilism of the essences*. To it is directed the ideology of technological scientism, whose advanced wing today is in the biological–genetic sector. The source from which this specific form of nihilism is nurtured lies in an emphatic raising of becoming alone, conjoined with the a priori negation of the necessary stratum of being and the assumption that essences are mere lexical conventions (*flatus vocis*), something that depends fundamentally on the choices of man and on the never firm determinations of his freedom. The gnoseological–ontological anti-realism here takes the form of unreality of essences/natures. Given that this negation is postulated and therefore illusory, it appears to the scrutiny of the intellect to be condemned to failure, as well as being dangerous, since many negative results could flow from the attempt to violate the inviolable. For this reason *Fides et Ratio* shows itself clear-sighted in its invitation not to stop at the way language expresses and understands reality, but to go further in verifying the ability of reason to discover essences.

Coordinated with this position defined as 'nihilism of the essences' is the attack on the idea of *substance* in an attempt to resolve it into that of function, as in the case of Kelsen. An inner necessity links theoretical nihilism as oblivion of being with the abandonment of the concept of substance, as it is the first and fundamental expression of the real being: only individuals or individual substances exist.

If now, without losing sight of the speculative diagnosis, we pass to the practical field, we can speak of an ethical nihilism, understood as an attack on values, an attempt at their dissolution, relativism. The moral nihilism that

today constitutes perhaps the most evident component of the theme of
nihilism, by the frequency with which it is evoked in culture, possesses
some practical roots (as well as much else). To us it seems to originate in the
primacy of the negative over the positive, of eros over Agape, of the indirect–negative over the direct–positive. This nihilism, in which it is postulated that the positive stems from the negative, is paradigmatically matched
by Nietzsche's idea that the morality of love, of forgiveness, of mercy, is not
born of a positive heroic impulse of the person, but emerges as an
unconfessable disguise of a harsh feeling of resentment (*ressentiment*) towards life, strength and joy. [6]

It is not difficult to connect with this picture another remarkable meaning
of ethical nihilism, which stems from a weak, plural reason, sceptical and
resigned to decline. The 'soft' form of moral nihilism which seems to
prevail in the modern West, is rather like a form of 'do it yourself' and
originates in the metamorphosis of the criterion of autonomy, on which
modernity had staked its best cards. Maintaining that the supreme principle
of morality is autonomy as self-legislation of the reason, Kant (see
Grundlegung zur Metaphysik der Sitten) had before his mind a single moral
law and a single, universal and immutable self-legislation of the reason. But
what can be said today, when the one has become many, when the moral law
has crumbled into the unlimited plurality of the empirical self-legislations
of single individuals? Within this new spiritual climate both prohibiting and
prescribing become meaningless.[7]

To reveal frankly here our conviction, it seems to us that in so many
forms of speculative nihilism a leading part is played by an intimately anti-
realistic, logico-dialectical formalism. Empty and sterile in real terms, it is
devoid of all sense of being. An absolute logicism reduces it to nullity.
Perhaps its origin can be discerned in the concealment of real being with
which the great and delusive machine of Hegelian dialectics is pregnant. On
this basis being, that which is richest and the most fully determinate, is seen
by the *science of logic* as the most empty, the poorest, the most indetermi-
nate, the pure nothing. Rarely in the history of philosophy has there been a
form of the oblivion of being of equal intensity. In the meanwhile it will
remain as a constantly revived question whether it is ever possible to grasp
reality while remaining enclosed within a grid of merely logical concepts.
Within logicist nihilism circulates, to a greater or lesser degree, a feeling of
contempt for reality: perhaps it appears too humble in the eyes of the
doctors of logic for them to pause and consider it.

(Some aspects of the relationship between nihilism, the criticism of
ontotheology and *analogia entis* are developed in Appendix II.)

Attempts at Liberation from Nihilism

If technological scientism – for which 'to be/being' in the highest sense
does not signify 'to be forever/always being' but only 'to remain in the
presence, ready for every transformation' – reveals itself as an important

trait of nihilism, it does not seem to us that the existentialist philosophies, those of freedom or the transcendental ones, are capable of achieving the desired escape from it. Often existentialism hangs existence on an act of freedom and ultimately on the abyss of freedom (the term is symptomatic), that is, in the last resort, on a *decision*. The existentialist, understanding that one cannot dwell endlessly in relativism and nihilism, decides to emerge from it by an act of freedom. The problem does not consist in escaping from relativism or nihilism, but in the way we do it.

Perhaps the most inward character of existentialism is its awareness that at the bottom of all knowledge and of ourselves we discover the abyss, that-which-is-not-founded. It is so radical that it threatens the Absolute itself, so that in the last analysis all truth and meaning rest on the unfounded abyss of freedom, human or divine, as the case may be, but the original structure of the reality is not altered. If all meaning comes from the obscure and 'principial' (that is, that which has reference to the principle) act of freedom, then all meaning is founded on a decision and ultimately there is no such thing as meaning but only decision. Despite differences of personal intention, existentialism of this kind, which contains a misunderstanding of the essence of freedom and of the ultimate nature of being, does not seem capable of checking the progress of nihilism.

If we look at it from the aspect of transcendental philosophy, which taken as a whole has constituted the ontology of the moderns, we find it contains many things worthy of respect, but not being. One finds things and men, *onta* and human subjects, and certainly the 'anthropological difference' between the inanimate *onta* and living, thinking man. In fact subjectivity is raised so high that modern transcendental doctrine could hardly have been born outside the all-embracing doctrine of anthropocentrism, in which – according to Barth – man is the universal subject and Christ at best the predicate. Such a philosophy could have been a philosophy of consciousness and of freedom, and it was both of these things together. Yet it failed to produce that openness of the soul to the whole, without which it is impossible to break out of nihilism. The openness of the soul, expressed in the ancient adage, *anima est quodammodo omnia*, here signifies openness to being and to experience, in the possible acceptance of that infinite openness produced in us by Revelation. Nietzsche had profound reasons for seeking with unflagging energy to abolish the soul as ontological and theological sensorium. Oblivion of being and of the soul and dissolution of ethics go hand-in-hand.

Two great and vital currents seem available to help us to break out of nihilism: *the philosophy of being and the biblical tradition*. Without concerning itself with questions which are left to discussion among different philosophical currents, the encyclical suggests that one of the major limits of modern philosophy lies in having put being in brackets, in not having been able to present itself as philosophy of being.[8] Consequently it has encountered greater difficulties in rediscovering the proper wisdom that is peculiar to philosophical thought, going towards the fragmentation of knowledge (cf. nn.83, 97, the latter a pivot of the whole discussion). With reference to metaphysics, we are justified in evoking by contrast that area of modern philosophy that defines itself as post-metaphysical, in allusion to the irreversible devaluation of the foundations of the true and valid which it sees in Western culture. The diagnosis remains problematic as to its speculative value; it does, however, confirm the precariousness of finding any meaning and preserving the content of moral insights when thought methodically separates itself from ontotheology and from religion.

Having already spoken of the philosophy of being, let us now take a look at religion, biblical tradition and Revelation.

Knowledge of God and Earthly Goals

Implied in the general relationship between philosophy and religion are many complex problems. In this section, as well as the next one, we would like to take a look at three of them: (a) whether or not the knowledge of God should be today considered an extraphilosophic problem; (b) in what the task of 'philosophy of religion' consists, (c) whether or not there exists an insuperable difference between philosophy and religion so that a 'philosophical religion' would be an equivocation.

In a secularized West there is a rather widespread idea that knowledge regarding God does not belong to the culture by now definitely involved in worldly goals. That is something best left to the realm of private sentiment and what does not constitute knowledge. Analogous opinions sometimes circulate regarding the Bible which is acknowledged as the 'great Codex' from which the Western spirit has continued to draw sustenance for many centuries, but which is now considered surpassed, together with Christianity. An influential part of the culture of Western people looks forward to a postmodern environment which assumes the forms of a post-metaphysical, post-biblical and post-Christian era. In the process something decisive emerges, so that, in the relationship between Western culture and Christianity, the problem most worthy of being reflected upon is whether the first can really do without the second, while it remains true that Christianity can do without Western culture. This of course assumes the great inadequacy of a secularized and laicized Christianity, often the precursor of atheism. Thus once again there is a choice to be made for or against Christianity.

At this crossroads we meet the most arduous problem for present-day culture and theology: how to reconcile within existence free human goals, endowed with autonomy and determination, with a religious conscience. And how to do it in such a way that those goals, in the multiple variety of their worldly aspects, are fecundated by the divine and brought back to it. It remains one of the most important tasks of religions, especially of Christianity within the era of late modernity, to reconcile the position of worldly goals with religious knowledge and prayer, so that these are not rendered irrelevant by the increasing extension of worldly activities, which constitutes the spirit of the Enlightenment. Which is the proper balance between knowledge of God and earthly knowledge with its goals? And how does one achieve it within the present explosion of mundane knowledge? The answer does not seem to be possible within the mere ethical realm which in itself is the norm of the worldly; that would imply accepting the challenge on the favoured field of the Enlightenment, where with a choice laden with important consequences God is considered an aspect no longer pertinent to philosophy and prejudicially kept at the margins.

Be that as it may, the problem is real. While religion teaches that God has created everything, the subject sees now that it is man that has done and has continued doing everything through the multiplicity of his earthly praxis. The crisis of religious consciousness originates from its deprivation of the perception of God's activity. It is as if He were only on a far corner of a polygon while man occupies all the others. Conscience therefore remains in a sundered state: while it *believes* that everything is made by God, it *sees* at the same time that everything is made by man, so that the subject's very feeling of his dependency vanishes. The autonomy of the praxis tends to feed on the destruction of the religious sense and to separate itself from the truth of things, according to which the authenticity of what is worldly rests on the divine.

Christian conscience can answer by discerning, among mundane aims, the ones which are assumable under a transcendent viewpoint looking for reconciliation. Reconciliation is the word of Christianity: of the human and divine, of the intellect and of the heart, of freedom and grace. Reconciliation is a theological event, something that places God within the issue, not only an act which belongs to the mere moral order, as seems to happen in Hegel: 'within the ethical there exists and is fulfilled a reconciliation of religion with the worldly, with reality'.[9] A revealing statement! Within this Hegelian form of reconciliation the theological element seems to have vanished, replaced by the ethical. Since it establishes the universal, while the event of Christ is placed on the side of singularity, that kind of reconciliation is problematic because in it the fundamental actor remains excluded from the picture.

Although Hegel individuates lucidly the problem of Christianity's conciliation with a modern culture which seems not to need God and remains outside religion, his proposed solution, which attempts to hold together finite knowledge and religious sentiment, the finite and the infinite, remains dubious because religious consciousness is placed below philosophical consciousness (we will return to this subject). Concerning the Enlightenment, it has hardly ever attempted the road of reconciliation, much preferring the method of separation (*aut-aut*). It resolves the conflict between intelligence and religion by simply abandoning religion, that is, letting go of one pole and holding on to just one. This way, however, the spirit remains in turmoil and strife: if I neglect religion I will eventually reach religious indifference, which is often the legacy of superficial souls. If I hold on to religious sentiments and reject the worldly, I run the danger of holding on to a dividing wall between one and the other and consequently the spirit will not assume a fundamental interest in religion. Neither option is recommendable: neither reconciles authentically because they both leave out some essential elements, among them mystical experience and the possibility of a revelation.

Philosophy of Religion and Revelation

Religion is still considered nowadays, but we question ourselves less and less on the philosophy of religion: its very identity seems to have become problematic. We do know that it is an academic discipline that is tradition- ally inserted within the realm of moral and anthropological disciplines – a curious but revelatory attribute, because it suggests the idea that religion belongs to or is one and the same as morality. This collocation raises the general question as to whether or not the philosophy of religion possesses enough credentials to even exist as an autonomous discipline capable of founding itself epistemologically.

In order to clarify in a preliminary way this important issue, we need to ask ourselves: What is the philosophy of religion and what does it deal with? It revolves around the knowledge about God that man is capable of reaching and his relationship with Him. The primary object of religion is God and man's relationship with Him. That is also the object of the philoso- phy of religion. Religion and philosophy of religion, but secondarily and always in reference to God and man, are both interested in cult, in religious practices, sacrifices and the sacred.[10]

Since the philosophy of religion revolves around a (natural) knowledge of God and man's relationship with Him through *religio*, which is at the very least piety and cult, it is not an autonomous discipline capable of founding itself; rather, it is valid as a section of metaphysics (and anthropology). It is in fact one of the tasks of metaphysics to investigate the impulse of man's reason towards God on two levels: within the framework of natural religion and without excluding the eventuality of a divine revelation. The possibility of an adequate philosophy of religion that does not stop at phenomenological investigation into the sacred, the religious, the numinous, rests on metaphys- ics, that is, on the capacity of the intellect to transcend the realm of the empirical in order to journey into the meta-empirical.

Having introduced the terms of the problem it is easier to intuit that the philosophy of religion has also been involved in the crisis of metaphysics, to the point that it lacks its own proper object and has to rely on phenomenological elements which can be useful and propaedeutic but not decisive. If the object of the philosophy of religion is religion, understood as revolving around God and man's relationship with Him, then the discipline may be in danger of ending up in a disaster inasmuch as God, for centuries now, is no longer an object about which philosophy thinks it can affirm or negate anything. It considers Him unreachable, unknowable, something be- yond the reach of the intellect. From this situation springs the attempt to change the very object of the discipline, which invents for itself new objects as it goes along, depending on the trends of the times, with a preference for the sacred or trying to attribute maximum value to the religious behaviour of man, but with a bad conscience, since the immense Object is never reached and that behaviour consequently is addressed to an 'x'. All this is said without in any way denigrating the considerable contributions which have been offered by religious sociology and psychology, as well as by cultural anthropology which studies the religious habits of people.

The fact that for a long while now philosophy turns towards God with increasing hesitation was recognized almost two centuries ago by Hegel with these powerful words: 'There was a time when the whole of science was a science of God. Our era, on the contrary, can be characterized above all by the fact that it knows an infinite number of objects and nothing at all about God.'[11] The proliferation of specialized knowledge revolving around the finite has drastically reduced the area of knowledge about God. It is no longer strange that one knows nothing about God: on the contrary, proceeding *etsi Deus non daretur* is elevated to a methodological universal principle. Nevertheless, our purpose as philosophers, the very goal towards which we aim, is that of knowing being and, through being, God: not God as He is in his eternal essence, but at the very least that He exists; to know Him from far away, in the mist, indirectly through his created mirrors. That is the concern of the highest part of metaphysics as well as that of philosophy of religion.

The highest concept of God that metaphysics, understood as natural theology, and the philosophy of religion can formulate is that of God as *ipsum esse per se subsistens*. God as being: that is a notion to which we can attain naturally. And with that notion we can attain to God as spirit and as thought, able to manifest Himself as *Deus absconditus* (a hidden God). This is the crucial hinge connecting metaphysics and philosophy of religion and which remains open to a possible Revelation. Since it is connected and dependent on metaphysics, the philosophy of religion cannot presuppose its object. Hence it finds itself in a more difficult condition than that of revealed Christian theology, which accepts its content from faith and Revelation. At this crossing comes forward the support of *Fides et Ratio*. By proclaiming the natural knowledge of God by the human intellect (and by metaphysics as a discipline), and by reconstituting its object (about the other side of its object, that is, man, there is no doubt), it makes possible once again the philosophy of religion. Not only that, it also suggests that it constitutes itself as an open discipline – open, that is, to a possible Revelation and therefore ready to complete itself as an anthropological metaphysics which individuates in man the radical ability to remain in wait for the hearing of a possible Revelation, should it happen. Thus the philosophy of religion, which is essentially a natural theology in union with an anthropological metaphysics, takes the position of a *praeparatio evangelica* in relation to the more general task of evangelical preparation concerning the whole of philosophy.

We have mentioned in Chapter 1 that the other focal point of the encyclical (perhaps less developed than the one revolving around philosophy and its claim to truth) is the problem of Revelation without which there is no Christianity. *Revelation is by its intrinsic nature a self-revelation*. In fact, when God reveals, He reveals nothing but Himself. He communicates

Himself and His greatest self-communication is that of sharing His son with men. Before being a divine suggestion to man, a help for the journey of a limping reason, Revelation is essentially a self-Revelation, which is at the same time a revealing and a doubling of the veil, according to the double meaning of *re-velatio*, in which occurs God's dialectic: He reveals Himself by hiding Himself, and He hides Himself in His Revelation. Revelation as *veritas semper indaganda* emerges as the place of contact and of confrontation between philosophical thinking and theological thinking (see n.79), within a kind of circularity through which philosophy is guided by God's word towards new objects, and theology attends to the development of faith's understanding, asking and receiving the help of reason's energy.

A hint that here we may have touched the most delicate nerve of the relationship between Christianity and modernity is the fact that two ecumenical councils within the span of one century attended to Revelation and dedicated to it their most important dogmatic constitutions: *Dei Filius* of Vatican I and *Dei Verbum* of Vatican II. Even today the issue is crucial and in this regard the Jewish philosophers (Buber, Rosenzweig, Lévinas) best elucidate its importance. A reflection on Revelation is something we cannot shirk, keeping in mind the two poles within which it takes place: that of man, inasmuch as he can potentially be a listener to a word that may be addressed to him by God,[12] and that of God since He may freely decide to speak by carrying out an action which is a gratuitous self-communication to man; that is, grace.[13]

Here we might employ the term 'philosophy of Revelation', thus clarifying its significance. Theology is not born by having a philosophical look at theological objects, but rather by operating within a movement wherein the instrument of knowledge is faith, while philosophy carries out a task of cooperation by which it is elevated and almost 'transubstantiated'. Aquinas writes that 'Qui utuntur philosophicis documentis in sacra Scriptura redigendo in obsequium fidei, non miscent aquam vino, sed convertunt aquam in vinum' (Those who employ in the Holy Scripture philosophical documents, bringing them in faith obedience, do not mix water with wine, but transform water into wine).[14]

When the idea of a Revelation is not abolished a priori, but remains an open possibility, then the idea is established that it can bring something new to man and to his mind, disclosing to him unexplored realms. One of the most significant sentences of the encyclical, perhaps the most pregnant and characteristic, is this: 'Revelation introduces into our history a universal and ultimate truth which stirs human mind to ceaseless effort' (n.14). To open oneself to Revelation is to open oneself to the Incarnation, to the cross. There is a powerful stimulus to philosophical thinking in the *Verbum caro factum est* and the *In cruce unus de Trinitate mortuus est*. Taking a stance of openness towards a possible Revelation within history, reason does not contradict itself, rather it takes up a stance of critical listening for something which could stimulate it and give it a tension that would allow it to express its optimal yield: in other words, something that puts the subject in motion for a never-ending journey, in which also theoretical contemplation has its place. At the risk of offending rationalist ears, we cannot fail to mention here the inexhaustible speculative solicitations which can be derived from the content of dogma. Altogether we can now easily understand how *Fides et Ratio* invalidates the idealistic and neo-idealistic thesis according to which religion constitutes an inferior form of philosophy, because it knows as myth and representation what philosophical knowledge knows as conceptually and consciously expressed truth.

In this regard we encounter some difficulties raised by present-day thought. Today it rarely declares itself explicitly atheistic; rather it stays strictly within the finite and, when it turns toward the divine, it understands it in two ways: (a) at times in the version of a polyvalent presence of the divine as in paganism, that is, within a propensity towards polytheism: not God but the gods, the pantheon; or (b) within the categories of deism, as a faraway God, indifferent to human history, expelled from the world and not acting on it. Consequently the essence of religion becomes ethics as interested in inter-human relationships. Within this instance one prescinds from any knowledge that may come from God, implying that such knowledge does not constitute a fulfilment of any kind, neither is it something relevant for the management of life. In relationship to ethics the idea is then developed of a minimum moral common denominator, a sort of universal ethics, which claims to be more valid and higher than religious confessions, placed at the same level and assessed as equivalent by an intrinsic pluralism. By considering philosophical truth a path which prepares for and leads to the acceptance of Revelation, *Fides et Ratio* invites us to take up again the study of God as the highest object of knowledge: God as being, spirit, love; a God who reveals Himself and lives in His people.

Philosophical Religion or Religious Philosophy?

While a philosophy of religion (with the above-mentioned caveats) is legitimate, and so is a *religious philosophy* capable of being inspired by and of integrating in its fabric the religious element, a *philosophical religion*, understood according to paradigms devised by Hegel and Gentile, has little foundation: these are philosophies that wholly incorporate within the movement of reason the transcendent content of religion, digesting it, dissolving it within their speculation, at best letting it alone for the use of ordinary uneducated people. This approach eliminates faith as a source of knowledge distinct from mere reason. But there are no reasons to think of philosophy as the supreme and complete exposition of an absolute system of truth, as both Hegel and Gentile thought. If we look at Gentile we will see that his constant position was that myth resolves itself in reason, and religion in philosophy. He never renounced his understanding of actualism as a kind of thought capable of 'reducing' art and religion, or his appraisal of religion as, at best, an inferior kind of philosophy (*philosophia inferior*) which must remain such and therefore stay away from any attempt at modernization and renewal (that explains his strong opposition to Catholic modernism), or else it must transcend and transform itself in philosophy. Religion for Gentile begins where the critical process of reason stops. Revelation can reveal nothing that reason does not already know.[15]

We would like to demonstrate now that philosophical religion – understood as one with an immanent genesis of all its content from reason, with a full resolution of its content in the concept – is an equivocation. To trace the parameters of its impossibility we must invoke the profound life of the self, that subjectivity which is such because of its mystery and its profundity, without forgetting that any of God's messages to man are first addressed to his subjectivity, to that precariousness that the self carries within himself, to that puzzling mystery that is the individual, every individual. Religion, and in a very special way Christianity, is an ultimately non-objectifiable relationship between two persons, between an interiority and another interiority, between the human subject and the divine Subject; *it is all in the relationship among subjects*. God is a 'Thou' not a 'him' or, worse, an 'it'.

Our first affirmation will be this: individual subjectivity and its profound experience, within which the religious phenomenon shows itself, is ultimately to be placed outside the grasp of the concept and therefore outside the grasp of philosophy. The concept is by its own nature objectifying; that is, *it knows subjects as objects*: to know through the concept means to objectify, to universalize, to go in the opposite direction of knowledge of the individual subjectivity as such. Conceptual knowledge, which is necessary and indispensable, pays a high price in not being able to reach the subject in its individuality. If the mystery of subjectivity is unreachable by the knowledge through the concept, it is also unreachable by philosophy; it is outside it.

> The unsurmountable limitation against which philosophy finds itself is due to the fact that it knows without any doubt subjects but it knows them as objects, it is completely within the relationship intelligence–object, while religion is within the relationship between subject and subject. That is why every philosophical religion and every philosophy which claims, as Hegel's does, to assume within itself and to integrate religion, is in the final analysis a mystification.[16]

Within a philosophical religion the relationship to God is not an interpersonal relationship, where God is before man and the two subjects can communicate.[17]

Beyond this objectifying knowledge reached through the concept, there is a non-objectifying kind of knowledge of subjectivity which can reach the subjectivity of another individual. It moves on the wings of empathy, of connaturality and love. This kind of knowledge, understood as a non-alienating relationship, meets the requirements of a very profound desire on the part of the subject of not losing one's self, of finding a meaning in life, *and to be recognized*: that there may be someone in the world or out of it who recognizes me in my wounded and precarious individuality; someone who knows me better than I know myself, who looks with mercy and renders me justice. Perhaps man can do without the desire to be happy, but he cannot renounce that of being recognized, or the desire that somebody should render him justice. Hell is not being recognized by anybody.

Beyond a deluded philosophical religion, faith and philosophy have much to communicate to each other. Here we can recall a famous thought by Adorno as a way of stimulating this reflection. It concludes his *Minima Moralia*:

> The kind of philosophy which alone can justify itself face to face with despair, is the attempt to consider all things the way they would show themselves from the standpoint of redemption. Knowledge has no other light but that which emanates from the redemption of the world: everything else ends in an a posteriori construction and belongs to technique. It is a question of establishing the perspectives within which the world disarranges, estranges itself, reveals its cracks and crevices as it will one day appear, deformed and lacking under the messianic light.[18]

There is a great divergence here between the perspective of this passage of Adorno and the idea of a strictly philosophical religion. How can they communicate with each other? Perhaps through the question of death which is implicit in Adorno and which philosophy cannot avoid. Here one remembers Gentile once again and his reflections on death which close *Genesi e struttura della società* (Origin and Structure of Society). The two perspectives communicate on the question of death even if they confront it differently. If we investigate their reasons, the answer would be this: within a rationalistic philosophical religion there is no real overcoming of death. That kind of philosophy either avoids the problem of death or places it in the background, resorting to the cruel assertion that 'everything that exists deserves to die (or is worthy of death)', by which according to Engels one would recognize the powerful and authentic soul of Hegelian dialectic. Here we have not a simple awareness of the general declining and the vanishing of entities, but a universal law; that is, the *deserved and due destination of everything to death*. With this reference to death as something ontologically deserved there appears the idea of existence as an *ontological fault* intrinsic to it rather than as an event which comes after because of a disobedience due to free will. Consequently philosophy, for which the theme of *meditatio mortis* seems to be something which it cannot do without, owing to the perspectives it can disclose and the question on the beyond that it can raise, runs the risk of being intrinsically tied to death, since it posits everything as worthy of death without exceptions and without residues of transcendence.

A philosophical religion pays the price of being satisfied with the enigma of evil, by bringing it back to a universal guilt and finally to the mortality of everything. In Adorno's statement appears a different perspective because he, without forgetting philosophy's task to relate to death, looks at it from the standpoint of redemption, in an attempt to consider being not only from the perspective of its declining and perishing, but also from the perspective of what could happen to it under the impact of the messianic redemption.

Postmodern Philosophy as 'Praeparatio Evangelica?' Five Characters

In the relationship between philosophical knowledge and Revelation two significant issues address us. First, can we generally think of philosophy as evangelical preparation (*praeparatio evangelica*), that is, as an area of knowledge predisposing one to the kind of listening which is open, friendly, not pre-judgmental of the Christian message? *Fides et Ratio* answers the question positively, basing itself on the experience of St Justin and of Clement Alessandrian (see n.38). Second, more particularly, can we consider postmodern philosophy within the horizon of *praeparatio evangelica*? Has not such a thought, in its numerous manifestations, declared itself atheistic or anti-theistic? Is it not currently on the road to nihilism, or at the very least does it not befriend it? Various indications and signs would suggest an affirmative answer to these questions.

On the other hand, it is not the philosopher's task to prepare the daily agenda for the future: it is enough that he carry the burden of the concept. We would already have made some progress if we could simply determine what we mean by evangelical preparation. In having recourse to this expression we are employing an ancient concept as employed by Clement Alexandrian, who understood Greek philosophy as a path and a journey that prepares one for the reception of the Gospel: something similar can also be found in Augustine in respect of Platonic philosophy (see *De civitate Dei*, 1, VIII). For Clement the 'Testament' utilized by the Gentiles was philosophy. It justified the Greeks who, according to Clement, in some way perceived the two fundamental truths about God as creator and providence of the universe. It needs to be remembered here that this thesis was disputed by the gnostics and the Marcionists, who understood philosophy as a diabolic sort of wisdom given to man by the fallen angels. Philosophy and knowledge were regarded as fruits of the snake.[19]

One can individuate this kind of philosophy which prepares the way for the announcement of the Gospel as a natural equivalent to the task of John the Baptist who prepared the way to the Word: he who prepares the way removes the major obstacles so that the journey be not tortuous. This idea of Clement could be valid today too, as long as we can identify the most urgent form of evangelical preparation which philosophy can offer. If I question myself on the issue I begin to see that this preparation should include a recovery of the sense of truth and of God, as well as the ability to remove from the ground the major obstacles, among which nihilism, which has shattered not only the idea that philosophy could be valid as *praeparatio evangelica*, but also another 'traditional' task which understands philosophy as a cure and a medicine for the soul.

In respect of Clement's horizon, which confronted the ancient world as it was before the coming of Christ, we of course live under different historical circumstances, since the Gospel has already been announced. Therefore the subject of a preparation by philosophy cannot be understood in a mode substitutive or surrogative of something that is not there yet, rather it should be understood in a cooperative and opening mode: to prepare for the journey by not placing obstacles in the way to something which has already manifested itself. In a more determinative fashion, this means that philosophy should not adulterate the sense of the true and of the good, and should so operate that the subject is steered in those directions.

In trying to understand how philosophy can undertake a task of evangelical preparation, there are different paths and methodologies which could be apt for the purpose. Our way will adopt a narrative method which, however, encompasses philosophical potentials. We will turn to characters of past history and will claim that from their example could issue a permanent inspiration for the understanding of evangelical preparation and the cooperation between faith and reason. We will choose persons who are capable of incarnating philosophy and faith in their purest form. Who is/are the representative(s) of philosophy? Who is/are the representative(s) of faith? We will recall before the mind's eye five characters: Socrates, Jesus, Pilate, Abraham and Odysseus/Ulysses, and will observe their behaviour.

Socrates has traditionally been recognized as the representative, and in some sense the father, of philosophy, worthy of the kind of love that the pupil Plato nurtured for him and that never failed, within that nostalgic wonder which one day surprised him in the encounter with the master. Even Nietzsche, who had an adversarial relationship with the cyclopic eye of Socrates, to which he attributed the dissolution of Greek tragedy and the birth, with philosophy, of a disproportionate theoretical optimism, recognizes Socrates' exceptional relevancy (see *The Birth of Tragedy*). In Jesus lives the eternal incarnate Word, or at the very least an exceptional personality, a great moral teacher, as Kant recognized. If we now observe attentively these two characters, similar in several aspects, something draws our attention and stimulates our reflection. Socrates *questions*, Christ *is questioned*. The Athenian goes around the public square, the agorà, asking questions and frequently irking his interlocutors, to whom he appeared to be an inopportune gadfly. He goes around asking questions such as What is justice? What is the good? What is happiness? Philosophy was born out of these questions, as well as those of the preceding Ionic philosophers. So Socrates questions. Jesus, on the other hand, is questioned along the byways of Galilee and Judaea. He is questioned by the Scribes, by the Pharisees, by the rich young man, by the people, by his mother, by the High Priest, by the apostles, by the disciples, and so on. He is questioned because he is expected, with his answers, to give testimony to the truth.

Socrates is not the truth, hence he questions. He questions to know and also to correct, by a critical dialogue, unfounded opinions. Christ's interlocutors intuit that in him there is something awesome and mysterious, perhaps truth itself; therefore they question him. He who questions does not know already. He is searching. He who gets questioned, already knows and is questioned on what he knows. This introduces a divergence between the two characters which is the difference between philosophy and the divine. Philosophy searches for God but it is not divine: it does not know but wants to know. To this search it dedicates its best efforts and rarely arrives at a condition of quietude. Here surfaces another difference as to the character of the questioning: Socrates asks questions with the purpose of arriving at the truth of ethical essences. Ultimately Christ gets questioned about himself: 'Who are you?' they ask him. They also ask him, 'What is truth?'

The question of identity and the question of truth come together and merge into each other. That was the question of Pilate during Jesus' trial. Pilate asks: 'What is truth?' (*quid est veritas?*), but does not wait for an answer. He is too busy. He is in a hurry to conclude the trial in any way whatever, so as not to displease too much those whose favour he courts and whose support he does not want to lose. He is perhaps the very prototype of so many important people who have always something urgent waiting for them and nothing really essential to do. Pilate is distracted and therefore does not bother to wait for an answer. He turns to the rabble and asks: 'What do you want that I should do with him?' He asks, but not in relation to the truth. Truth has no answer for those who are in a hurry.[20] If there is a teaching that stands out from the dialogue between Jesus and Pilate, it is the invitation to peace and quiet: to the reiteration of the question and the waiting for the answer with patience and perseverance. Socrates is tireless in his questioning, and his questioning is authentic, not fake and rhetorical. He is in no hurry. Perhaps he is a contemplative. As a matter of fact he is one, as the episode of Potidea attests. There, during a military campaign, he remained transfixed in uninterrupted reflection for a whole day and night, to the amazement of friends and soldiers (see *Symposium*, 220ff).

What should we think of Jesus, of Socrates and of Pilate? Jesus who is questioned on his divinity is beyond philosophy and faith. Socrates seems to be the representative of philosophy. Pilate is open to more than one interpretation. He is authority unfaithful to its task. Perhaps he is the curious who asks negligent questions, quite differently from the way Socrates asks them. While we have found the representative of philosophy, we have not yet found that of faith. It cannot be either Pilate or the Word Incarnate. As we have not recalled Abraham yet, the dialogue between philosophy and faith cannot go forward. Abraham is the father of all believers; he believed against all hope (*spes contra spem*). 'Abraham believed, therefore he is young, since he who always hopes for the best thing, he grows old because he will be disillusioned from life; he who always expects the worst, he will grow old prematurely; but he who believes retains an eternal youth,' wrote Kierkegaard in *Fear and Trembling*.

Our 'staging' could well come to a conclusion here, having determined who is the representative of philosophy and who is the knight of faith. However a scruple of faithfulness and adhesion to the events of history leads us not to stop at this already significant conclusion. It is our turn to ask now whether we can find in Socrates as father of philosophy and in Abraham as father of all believers some analogous, fundamental attitudes, so that by bringing closer the two characters we bring closer philosophy and faith.

In the behaviour of Socrates and Abraham, something special and capable of establishing a secret affinity between the two comes to the fore and surprises us. It is the obedience to a voice addressed to them and from whose listening issue two quite different outcomes. In order to obey the voice of conscience and not to disobey the laws of the *polis*, Socrates remains in jail in Athens, drinks the hemlock and confronts death. In order to obey God's voice, Abraham leaves his native land and goes forward. *One stays, the other goes.* One stays in jail, the other leaves behind his native place. One goes towards death, the other towards the unknown.

They both left a thing behind and took a thing with them. Socrates left behind his desire to go on living and took with him the hope of immortality and of being able to continue philosophizing in the Ades. Abraham, by his readiness to sacrifice Isaac, left behind all human standards of common sense and took faith with him: a faith that was pure and absolute, since no request of that kind, no sacrifice of his son was ever required of Socrates. However, they are both united by the fact that they both listened to a voice which spoke to them and they both obeyed it. It is the same voice that calls and speaks in every man. Neither Socrates nor Abraham criticized, refused or emptied out the appeal addressed to them: by submitting they tried to understand; they were far from the pride of a thought centred upon itself which repulses anything that does not fit its own measurements.

In culminating acts of their own existence, the representative of philosophy and the knight of faith considered that it was not possible to avoid obedience to a voice. They listened and they obeyed. So, with postmodern philosophy, even if scarred by so many sceptical turns and so many formalistic temptations, it can function as *praeparatio evangelica* if it is able to recover a point of contact with Socrates' testimony, listening to his teaching, without losing sight of that of Abraham. To find a point of contact once again can here mean two things: not to interrupt the search too soon and too cheaply, that is, not to be too easily satisfied, as Socrates was not too easily satisfied, in dialoguing about truth; not to lose sight of the fact that Socrates repudiates the accusation of atheism which Meleto and others raised against him. The father of philosophy was not an atheist: 'But here is the hour to go away: I to die, and you to live. Who of us goes towards the better part is obscure to everyone except God' (*Apology*). Socrates had intuited that being in the highest sense is being forever.

Now, if Socrates, as Kierkegaard thought (see his *The sickness unto death*) is at a higher stage than modern philosophy, should we not add that Abraham is at a higher stage than Socrates? He is at a higher stage not according to an order of merit but as to election, since Abraham intuited something of the mystery of the Cross. From Socrates it was requested that he accept the unjust death sentence of the city, from Abraham it was requested that he sacrifice his only son. From whom was more requested? To the man from whom more was demanded and a greater hope was requested, was given a presentiment of the Cross. In the Cross (and in the Incarnation) we have the culmination of Revelation which happens 'with events and words which are intimately connected' (*Dei Verbum*, n.2). Socrates and Abraham are great men and their greatness has deep analogies, but between them there is the Cross, of which Abraham has an obscure intuition when he consents to obey the request to sacrifice Isaac. No dialectical structure, no rational argumentation can take away that Cross because it is beyond the human and beyond philosophy.

But our journey is not over yet. Besides Jesus and Pilate, Socrates and Abraham, Odysseus/Ulysses also has something to tell us. Once again this character points towards Abraham, since they both went on a journey and confronted the unknown, albeit for different purposes: Abraham to get out of his native land, Ulysses to return there and once more dwell in the place which is origin and spring (*origo and fons*) of all that is good and of family sentiments. Abraham is impelled by God's calling, the Dantean Ulysses by a great desire for 'virtue and knowledge': there is with him a passionate thirst for knowledge, capable of challenging death itself and giving testimony to the natural desire to know. He too, like Socrates, is an image of philosophy which must always return to its origins. To accomplish this task, philosophy is compelled to carry out a long, risky journey. He is led not by a vain *curiositas*, but by a desire to know, to go beyond the pillars of Hercules. Ulysses has nothing of the Nietzschean *Übermensch*. He is a symbol of human research, of the philosophy without faith, which magnanimously and valiantly risks everything, while remaining ultimately unable, by its own unaided strength, to go beyond those pillars. What does this character have to teach us? In answering, I beg to differ from Lévinas, for whom there is in Odysseus the Greek a dubious element identifiable in his desire to return to his point of departure, that is, to origins. Lévinas understands this attitude as the paradigm of an isolated subjectivity, closed upon itself, identical with itself, perhaps indifferent to the other's face.

There is, however, another possible interpretation. Both Abraham, leaving his native town, and Odysseus, attempting to return to his, risked all for truth. Given the fact that no word of God was addressed to Odysseus, he had to journey and take decisions by his own wit, attentive to the eternal voice of nature and to those affections which powerfully impelled him to a return to his native land by overcoming numerous dangers. All by himself, he risked all for the truth of origin: *he won and he lost*. He won by holding on steadily to his desire for knowledge; on the other hand, he lost the challenge of the unknown. Perhaps this is philosophy's destiny: to walk part of the way of the journey but never the whole: to know something and to be ignorant of something. To be able to journey further, it must ally itself and unite its cognitive energy with that emanating from Revelation. When or how this will happen in the postmodern world we do not know, but we hope that philosophy will at least walk with its own strength and trample on the solid ground of being! That is the condition of conditions and it bears many names: realism, sense of being, intellectual intuition of being, and so on. A philosophy oriented in that direction is by its own intrinsic nature open to the transcendent; it conceives of man as structurally predisposed to listening for a possible Revelation and overcomes the narrow finitude of the criterion of immanence. At this point we could ask the delicate question as to which and how many are the contemporary philosophies who respect the above-mentioned conditions. When wonder before being is authentic, philosophy finds itself on the right ground to encounter the infinite wonder of the

Incarnation, of the God–man. On this threshold the *praeparatio evangelica* is over and gives way to the *itinerarium personae in Trinitatem* (the journey of the person in the Trinity).

One could ask why, in determining the concept of philosophy as *praeparatio evengelica*, we turned to ancient characters and not to postmodern authors. This attitude could involve two different positions, both regrettable: that we are not sufficiently informed about postmodern thought, or that this thought – oriented towards scepticism, historicism and criticism of the idea of truth – is not suitable to promote a real evangelical preparation. On this matter some short reflections were suggested at the end of the previous chapter. Here it is opportune to add that, except for some ethical positions, postmodern radical thinkers seem inhabited by an intense rage against reason and by an anti-realism which place them in the shadow of forgetfulness of being. Some of them maintain the death of philosophy, the final crisis of reason and the separation between faith and philosophy. Only in a very peculiar way, and perhaps as a dialectically negative approach, could *praeparatio evengelica* be conceived in this area. In a kind of apophatism faith should be born as a cry which climbs on the ruins of any human certainty. A different approach can be found in some scientists who ask about cosmos, its laws and origins, its evolution. They do not refuse to bring their research into contact with philosophy and theology. The problems that over the past three decades interested the dialogue between science and faith (such as the inadequacy of reductionism and of mechanicalism) do not constitute an evangelical preparation in a full sense, but at least do not contradict it.

To some extent *praeparatio evangelica* begins and ends up with the question on truth. The Pilate's question is vital: *quid es veritas?* He did not wait for the answer. Anyway a silent, wordless answer was given by the Tried, and it is the very same question of Pilate, only differently read. In fact the anagram of '*Quid est veritas*' is '*Est vir qui adest*'. Truth is Logos.

Parting Words

Among the several concluding remarks that could be presented, we will consider only two matters, concerning nihilism and the relation between philosophy and Revelation.

Nihilism

The Western secularized culture is rather deeply affected by nihilism: this culture spreads and circulates a new 'common sense' according to which the universe is deprived of any meaning and, if God exists, he remains totally hidden to our minds. As modern philosophy seldom goes beyond the border of the finite, an anguish, correlated to man's closing in the finiteness, affects the subjects living in the postmodern spiritual climate. In the realm of culture and of philosophical quest, the main challenge arising from nihilism concerns the very continuation of philosophy. With nihilism could occur not only a transformation of philosophy as provoked by linguistic and hermeneutic turn, but the end of philosophy as an enterprise aimed at the knowledge of truth and at a form of wisdom. In fact, with the advent of nihilism, the sapiential dimension inherent to philosophy is progressively dissolved, while the perspective according to which philosophy is seen as a vocation and an existential practice with deep resonances in personal life disappears.

At the end of this dialectics, starting from the removal of knowledge of being, reason becomes more and more a prisoner to itself: some Kantian ideas concerning the 'transcendental illusion' of reason could have prepared this attitude. Nihilism seems to be an internal parasite of reason and metaphysics, strong at the end of the 20th century when one of our greatest threats is the temptation to despair.

The essence of Christianity is threatened by nihilism. On a 'theologal' (not simply theological) level the inner and concealed meaning of nihilism could be man's limitation to this world, with the severing of his desires directed toward the infinite. This is a strong challenge for Christianity and Revelation, because their ultimate meaning is not merely salvation, which implies liberation from sin, but mainly and firstly to become similar to God, that is, deification (*deificatio* in Latin). With nihilism Chistianity is no longer understood as a faith which is centred upon the deification of man as a gift of God.

Breaking free from nihilism could be a kind of rebirth for philosophy, and for theology a resumption of its sapiential, contemplative function, now less deeply felt because of the weight of various factors, including the still onerous influence of Heideggerianism in theology and a certain philological positivism in the approach to the Bible. For this break-out to take place, a resumption of the dialogue between philosophy and Revelation is desirable.

The Relation between Philosophy and Revelation

But we do not know whether in the West (the land of broken symbols, as Tillich defined it) philosophy and Revelation will again communicate intimately, as Jaspers, among others, hoped for. According to him, 'The Bible and the biblical tradition are one of the bases of our philosophy.... Philosophical research in the West – like it or not – is always done with the Bible, even when one fights it'.[21] Here we can once again suggest and integrate the meaning of an open philosophy as already stated: an open philosophy is one which, aware of its limitations, reached through a rational and controllable process, remains willing to listen for a possible Revelation, for a word within history proclaimed by the Transcendent, without excluding the possibility that it could derive from the same a stimulus and a support to arrive more easily at its goal. It seems that here two legitimate things come together: one, usually granted, is that reason should question Revelation; the other is that reason is questioned by Revelation to ascertain whether Revelation can possibly make a contribution to the placing of philosophy back on track and thus opening up new horizons to its gaze. This kind of open philosophy would not introduce itself as a philosophical religion, whose serious limitations we have already dealt with, neither would it come across as a generically religious philosophy. An appropriate name, albeit historically laden with multiple meanings, could be that of Christian philosophy. It would be appropriate because it would remain open, not only to the religious phenomenon, but specifically to the Revelation of Christianity. At that point it would be possible again to revive the travail of the concept in philosophy and in theology, which finds itself somewhat weakened in the attempt to keep up with an excessively positive biblicism and with highly historical approaches to the task of theology.

With the reconnecting of a virtuous circular process between philosophy and Revelation we could then proceed towards the overcoming of a considerable mutual separation. The separation was the result of either theology presenting itself as the culmination and the totality of human knowledge, or of philosophy doing the same thing, especially within idealism, which appropriates within its system theological intentionalities.

The absorbing of one discipline within another, or the opposite, their mutual separation, represents an impoverishment which is still with us. In Italy this goes back to 1874, to the elimination of religious and theological sciences from the national university curriculum. That would explain the scanty and insufficient dialogue with the Bible within both culture and philosophy. The Bible, although not the whole of Revelation, remains the great Western and East European codex. It is in fact a solemn river that gathers the waters of innumerable sources: voices, doubts, praises, lamentations, protests, questions, answers. It is the book of the dialogue between man and God, the *acta* of God's initiative towards man. We usually read Esiod, Plato, Sophocles, Cicero, Virgil, but not Genesis, Luke, Paul or Clement. Why Homer and not John? Perhaps a profound educational revolution is advisable as regards the model of instruction adopted in Europe for several centuries. It was originally based on the classical Greco-Roman tradition, subsequently amplified to include the sciences and technology, but nevertheless ignoring the Bible.[22]

The integration of the paradigm would presuppose a different relationship with Scripture and Revelation; a revisiting which should not be limited to the historical–critical methodology, important, but also sterile and problematic in some aspects.[23] We envision therefore the opportunity of a listening to and a utilization of the Bible within philosophy, something similar to what some Jewish philosophers have done, at least in the sense that it not be regarded as a document closed on its past. The rarity of biblical influence on philosophical thinking constitutes an impoverishment which diminishes the possibility of something new, of a revolution necessary for the overcoming of the current impasse in philosophical thinking. During the past decades there has been an intense attack upon reason, an attempt to establish its finite character (which is not false) but also its insuperable limitation to the finite, so that it gets portrayed as something always relative, completely dependent on the context, incapable of reaching the universal. In fact the universal and the concept are debased to the level of the absolute particular, not excluding the 'ethnic'. This is the obstacle that present philosophy has to remove.

Notes

1 E. Jünger, 'Oltre la linea', in E. Jünger and M. Heidegger, *Oltre la linea*, Milan: Adelphi, 1989, p.57.

2 Reviewing the complex and desultory debate on nihilism, to which Italian philosophy has on various occasions made a contribution, it is difficult not to arrive at the conclusion that the term is heading towards an increasing semantic extenuation: if so many phenomena of the spirit are attributed to nihilism, the word becomes a *passe-partout* for all seasons, a rubber band which can be stretched in any direction. With this increasing extension goes a great obscurity in comprehension and definition. A similar experience could be traced back 50 years to the widespread use of the word 'existentialism'. With some justification, J.P. Sartre observed that, since too many heterogeneous currents claimed to be existentialist, the term 'existentialism' no longer meant anything. It had become a conventional reference, good for varied purposes, loaning a more or less fitting dress to very different *silhouettes*.

  In order not to end up in a similar situation, a first step would be that of considering nihilism a multifaceted event which would in turn postulate a multi-level hermeneutics suggesting to philosophy an attitude which would exclude claims of exclusivity or all-inclusiveness. There are important recurrences of nihilism in art, in the life of the spirit and of religion and perhaps even in mysticism, if we are to take as valid that, for some mystics, Nothingness is assumed to be the most pure and highest name of God. Already within those modest notes we can appreciate the evocative power and the semantic equivocation of the term.

3 An important nihilism of the object, inasmuch as it is external and extrapsychic, is present in Freud, especially with reference to the interpretations of dreams understood as a fact that is absolutely and intrinsically internal, an exclusive production of the individual. 'The dream is a completely asocial psychic product ... issuing from the interior of a person as a sort of compromise between the psychic forces that contend with each other there, it remains incomprehensible even to oneself.' The psychoanalytical interpretation of dreams as totally internal products risks being considered one of the most stubborn myths of the 20th century.

  An aspect of anti-nihilism is that of functioning as a *metaphysics of exteriority* and therefore of the real density of the object, not as a negation of the subject, since the highest form of existence is the personal one where the philosophy of being recognizes the greatest ontological profundity and mystery.

4 The fundamental philosophical opposition which occurs between realism and nihilism can be precisely individuated as an opposition between nihilism and the philosophy of being (the maximum outcome of realism): it individuated the most speculatively sensitive place in the relationship between what is immutable and what becomes, and in the problematic polar postulates concerning either the original and innocent characteristic of becoming, or the eternity of all and each individual being. Just as the essence of the position which absolutizes the 'becoming' consists in ignoring the search of an adequate cause of becoming, so the essence of 'eternism' consists in ignoring and rejecting, without a sufficient reason, the very idea of potentiality (*dynamis*). The attempt to rub out the *dynamis* is the equivocation of much of modern philosophy, especially in its rationalistic side. Even part of neoclassical thought has remained caught in such an equivocation, with grave consequences for its metaphysical vision.

5 M. Weber, *Il metodo delle scienze storico-sociali*, Milan: Mondadori, 1980, p.96.

6 According to Nietzsche, resentment (*ressentiment*) operates as an unconfessable motive at the root of the morality of love, mercy and forgiveness. These sentiments would

be descriptive of the 'rebellion of the slaves within morality', which begins 'when the resentment itself becomes creative and generates values; the resentment of those [weak] beings to whom the authentic reaction, that of action, is negated and therefore console themselves with an imaginary revenge', *Genealogia della morale*, Milan: Adelphi, 1988, p.251.

7 Within 'weak thought' there is a paradoxical co-presence of two refusals: one of stable truth, the other of the will to power. It partially picks up the heritage of Nietzsche, who said 'no' to the first but 'yes' to the second. In weak thought we have a partial Nietzschean position and therefore an incomplete kind of nihilism. With the intention of fighting the idea of truth goes an attitude of *pietas* towards man and of suspicion toward power. These feelings can perhaps function as prolegomenon for a liberation from nihilism, which would happen at the existential level, if not yet at a speculative level. The abandonment of nihilism would happen if the issue of the stable, unchanging truth were not judged a form of violence. This blame is not in any way connected to the essence of truth.

8 On the problem of nihilism, especially the theoretical kind, see our *Terza navigazione. Nichilismo e metafisica*. The volume is committed to the individuation of an adequate definition of nihilism, a definition passionately sought by Nietzsche, by Heidegger and others, but which ultimately escaped them. It is in grasping the nature or the essence of nihilism that one can recognize the propaedeutic and necessary step in order to begin the healing from its 'sickness'. It is easy to recognize the impossibility of liberating oneself from an event whose nature one ignores.

9 *Lezioni sulla filosofia della religione*, ed. E. Oberti and G. Borruso, Bologna: Zanichelli, 1974, vol. I, p.60.

10 According to Aquinas, religion is essentially concerned with man's relationship to God, towards whom man is naturally ordained (*religio importat ordinem ad Deum*), see *S.Th.*, II II, q.81, a.1.

11 *Lezioni sulla filosofia della religione*, vol. I, p.64.

12 'Man is the entity who within his own history must have his ears open for an eventual historical revelation of God through the human word' (K. Rahner, *Uditori della parola*, Turin: Borla, 1988, p.208). Also: 'Man is the entity who, by freely loving, finds himself before a God of a possible revelation. Man listens to the word or to the silence of God in the measure in which he, by freely loving, opens himself to the message of the word or the silence of the God of revelation' (p.136). A philosophy is open when in its fundamental anthropology it shows that man is always, that is, by nature, predisposed to listen to a possible Revelation.

13 'It was pleasing to God, in His goodness and wisdom, to reveal Himself and manifest the mystery of His will, by which men through Christ, Word incarnate, in the Holy Spirit, have access to the Father and are made participants of the divine nature. In fact through this revelation the invisible God in His great love speaks to men as if they were friends and dwells among them' (*Dei Verbum*, n.2).

14 *In Boetii de Trinitate*, q. II, a. 3, ad 5m.

15 In Hegel, the *re-velatio*, which reveals and veils, has simply become *Offenbarung*, open and full manifestation, so that the speculative concept of God as spirit allows one to know the intimate necessity that He reveal Himself: 'God reveals himself. To reveal oneself means a conversion of infinite subjectivity, a judgment of infinite form, self-determination, to be for another: this self-manifestation belongs to the very essence of spirit. A spirit that does not manifest itself is not a spirit. God as spirit is essentially this: to be for another, to manifest oneself' (*Lezioni sulla filosofia della religione*, vol. II, p.250). Religion understood as the place of the necessary manifestation of God cannot but dissolve the mystery, which is exactly the way by which one attempts to reach the *episteme* and thus destroy *sophia*.

16 J. Maritain, *Breve trattato dell'esistenza e dell'esistente*, Brescia: Morcelliana, 1965, p.58.

17 Taking a rather hard look, M. Buber writes that 'Philosophy begins with a decisive

prescinding from its concrete situation, i.e., with an elemental act of abstraction'
   L'eclisse di Dio, Milan: Comunità, 1983, p.56.
18 T.W. Adorno, *Minima Moralia*, Turin: Einaudi, 1954, p.235 f.
19 'Before the Lord's coming, philosophy was necessary for the Greek's justification,
   now it is useful to lead souls to God, since it is a propaedeutic for those who arrive at
   faith through demonstration ... God in fact is the cause of all beautiful things, but of
   some in a special manner, such as the Old and the New Testament, and of others in a
   secondary manner, such as philosophy. And perhaps philosophy was a gift especially
   for the Greeks before the Lord would call them also: since it led the Greeks to Christ as
   the Law does for the Hebrew. Now philosophy remains as a preparation which places
   on the right path he who is perfected by Christ himself' (Clement, *Stromata*, 1 (5), 28).
   We should add here that in Clement's view the Greeks learned many doctrines from the
   Jewish prophets.
20 The question of Pilate – What is truth? – is not badly or inappropriately put: it was in
   fact *the* question. We must chide Pilate as a man and as a philosopher, not because he
   raised the question, but for not having waited for an answer. It would not be too daring
   to conjecture on what Jesus would have answered had Pilate really been interested in
   the issue: I am the truth, or else: do as I do; conform yourself to my person. This
   possible answer of Jesus confirms the idea of truth as conformity or adequation,
   expanding it beyond the still necessary declarative element.
21 K. Jaspers, *La foi philosophique*, Paris: Plon, 1952, p.129.
22 In the opus *Le poète et la Bible* (Paris: Gallimard, 1999), where the writings on the
   Bible by Claudel have been gathered, we read: 'Is it not an anomaly, from a purely
   cultural viewpoint, that the Bible should not occupy any space in the education of our
   college students when we impose on our poor lads the dullness of Orace Flacco and
   force them to admire, recalcitrantly, the great men of Plutarch who for the most part are
   little more than foul marionettes?' (*Avvenire*, 24 January 1999).
23 When such a method is understood as 'History of the Forms' (R. Bultmann), then the
   Jesus of history and the Jesus of faith part ways, arriving at a variant of Docetism so
   that at the origins of Christianity there are fewer and fewer facts and persons and more
   and more mythical projections of the community.

On the Concept of Truth in 20th-century Philosophy: Maritain, Wittgenstein and Heidegger

Let us try to look in some depth at the concept of truth, meditating on the lesson of three great philosophers of the 20th century: Maritain, Wittgenstein and Heidegger. Beyond the significant biographical similarities which bring together these three thinkers – the first was born in 1882, the other two in 1889 – it is the approach they had towards the issue of truth and metaphysics that demands a comparison, albeit a summary one, of their doctrines. Objectively, they had before them the challenge to which Nietzsche's pen had given literary expression. After asking 'What is truth?' he had furnished this answer:

> A mobile army of metaphors, metonyms, anthropomorphism, in short a sum of human relations which have been empowered poetically and rhetorically, which have been transferred and beautified, and that after long use appear to a people to be solid, canonical and binding: truths are illusions of which we have forgotten the illusory nature; they are metaphors which have been worn out and have lost all sensible strength; they are coins whose image is worn and are therefore valued only as mere metal, not as coins.[1]

This crude denunciation, although not argued (as is often the case in Nietzsche), is a picture that cannot be undervalued; a picture that will powerfully affect many postmoderns.

Maritain

The meditation on the nature of truth, understood within the noetic framework of the concept of conformity (*adaequatio*), occupied constantly the thought of this French philosopher: among the many treatises the ones treating the argument most explicitly are *Reflections on Intelligence* and *The Degrees of Knowledge*, wherein the truth (of an assertion) is reached within judgment and determined as 'the conformity between the act of the spirit which unites two concepts in one judgment, and the existence (actual or possible) of one thing within which those two concepts are realized',[2] or also according to the formula: 'When the identification operated from the spirit between two terms of a proposition corresponds to an identity within the thing, then the spirit is true.'[3] Therefore there is a declarative truth if the objects of thought carried within the subject and the predicate – different from each other and terms of distinct cognitive relations – when compared in a proposition, are identified in the thing and are realized in it. Indeed, while different notional objects cannot be identical with each other, a notional object can be identical to a thing to which another notional object is identical. Within the judgment 'Peter is white' the notions 'Peter' and 'white' are different, and yet they are both identifiable in the thing 'Peter'. By bringing up-to-date the classical lesson, Maritain attributes a key role to judgment: its task consists in allowing the spirit to pass from the level of simple essence (or of the notion presented to thought) to the level of the thing or of the subject which exercises existence. Judgment returns to the thing (or to the 'transobjective subject', according to the lexicon adopted by Maritain in *The Degrees of Knowledge*) its unity which simple apprehension, gathering different objects of thought, had pulled apart. Here the fully existential function of judgment is recalled, in the sense that it is with it and through it that the intellect 'grasps' existence.

Conformity between the intellect and the thing, which is the proper act of the mind within judgment, assumes (intentional) identity between thought and thing in the ante-predicative moment. 'In the act of knowing, the thing (in as much as it is known) and thought are not only united, but are also rigorously one: intelligence in act, as Aristotle puts it, is the intelligible in act.'[4] In any event, thought is not a copy or a mould of the thing, so that all the determinations of one are the determinations of the other. Otherwise where would error reside? One needs to introduce a sort of disjunction between the thing and thought: things are within thought not in an entitative mode but in an intentional mode. Out of this disjunction is born the possibility of error. At the same time, however, one must affirm the profound unity between thought and being, in the sense that knowledge is knowledge of being and it is reached in the concept: the end or terminal object of conceptual knowledge is the thing itself, present entitatively in the real and intentionally in the intellect. Thus the question posed by Kant regarding the relation between the representation within the mind and the thing outside the mind receives an answer. Kant, who often limited his cognitive ray to German to a post-Leibnizian or post-Wolfian sort of scholasticism, does not seem to know what precedes them and the various positions regarding intentionality. We should add here that within the idea of truth as conformity is implied that of an active moving of the intellect, of a never-ending dynamism, of a perpetual unrest, which aims at knowing being better and better. Moreover, the *res* thing is not only a material thing: that would be a rather gross understanding of the term '*res*'. Realism is not materialism or 'thingism'.

Wittgenstein

If now we turn our reflection to the *Tractatus*, it becomes evident that this author has perceived the central issues of the question of truth, taking a decisive step without, however, arriving at a final clear clarification of the issue. The *Tractatus* grasps the necessity of the existence of something identical (*identisch*) between notional image and reality in order to speak of truth within the relation of representation between image and things, as can be gathered from the propositions that go from 2.12 to 2.174 and that we partly transcribe in the note.[5] To my knowledge, these particularly significant expressions by Wittgenstein do not seem to have received the attention that they deserve. To some extent, the author himself has failed to give them full value. His interpreters, in harmony with the great focus given to the contemporary philosophy of language, have preferred to concentrate on linguistic analysis and linguistic games in Wittgenstein. Nevertheless, in the propositions of the *Tractatus* we have mentioned, the term 'language' does not appear. Rather they deal with the problem of the relation of representation between the mental–logic image and reality (existence). Assertion 2.161 uses the term '*identisch*', declaring that there must be something identical in the relation of representation between mental image and the real represented. One can easily see that in Wittgenstein the problem of intentionality receives a preliminary elaboration which is close to those of Maritain, of Aristotle and of the philosophy of being.

Nevertheless Wittgenstein seemed to recognize the *identisch* not within intentional identity between thought and thing in the concept: he individuated the possibility of a commonality between image and reality in the logical structure (cf. 2.19), so that in the final analysis logic can represent the world. Putting the emphasis on the logical structure rather than on the mind's act which intentions the thing within the concept in a relation of intentional identity, the *Tractatus* fails to arrive a full disclosure of the concept of truth and of the relation of thought to things which is rather summarily brought within the frame of logic. We may express this briefly as follows: it was grasped that the nature of true thinking requires that some form of *ante-predicative identity* be realized; but that identity was interpreted and traced back to logical structure. An essential step was taken, but the problem was not ultimately solved.

Heidegger

It is common knowledge that Heidegger recognized truth as *adaequatio*, understood as exactitude and accuracy of the judgment (*orthotes*), but to a great extent he subordinated it to truth as disclosure (*a-letheia*), as non-hiddenness, tying this idea to the image of the 'clearing'/*Lichtung*: 'It is only the *Aletheia*, the disclosure thought as *Lichtung*, that permits the possibility of truth ... the *Aletheia*, the non-hiddenness in the sense of a clearing of Openness where presence is revealed, was experienced immediately and only as *orthotes*, as exactitute in representing and rightness of enunciation.'[6] In clarifying the double modality of truth, Heidegger displays a lexicon which is itself dualistic, where *Aletheia* and *Lichtung* represent truth as disclosure, and *veritas* and *Wahrheit* denote declarative or apophantic truth, understood reductively as correctness or exactitude of enunciation.

While it is a plausible hypothesis that, within the non-hiddenness of the Heideggerian *Aletheia*, there is a reference to the existence of things, to their phenomenological autorevelation, within this hypothesis neither the problem of 'to whom?', which is to say of the subject to whom it manifests itself, nor that of thought are considered. Heideggerian reflection on the truth of being, in the dual sense of the subjective genitive (truth that belongs to being or ontological truth) and of the objective genitive (truth that is expressed on being or declarative truth), does not consider the thought and the axiom according to which, in order that there be a truth, there must be a thought that thinks it.

After reflecting on the dense pages of *On the Essence of Truth*, one can assert that Heidegger thought long and hard about the question of truth without ever reaching a positive conclusion because he never took the decisive step: that of recognizing, as happened with Wittgenstein, that in the ante-predicative moment there is some kind of identity between thought and reality. Heidegger intuited the relevance of the problem without being able to resolve it, arriving ultimately at the attempt – itself destined to be checkmated – to change the essence of truth: 'In the history of being the event (*Ereignis*) manifests itself to humankind first as a change of the essence of truth.'[7] With the abandonment of the determination of the *adaequatio*, which Heidegger could no longer accept, having lost its antecedents which render it valid and necessary, a 'new' determination of truth is adopted: 'the essence of truth is freedom',[8] which consists in letting being be. Freedom, by giving space to being, allows for its revelation: here surfaces the ancient phenomenological heritage of Heidegger, within which one lives within a horizon which is similar to the first of the three modalities of truth. In it being is not an object of a conceptual grasping.

Once intentional identity between the intellect and the thing within the concept, as well as the identity between image and reality which logic suggests, are precluded, Heideggerian reflection grasps that between the realm of thought and the realm of the real there must be some kind of 'bridge', in order to posit the problem of truth: 'How can one understand ontologically the relation between the ideal moment and the real moment?' Here, with barely different words, Kant's question and the problem of intentionality are resurrected. Nevertheless the nature of such a bridge was not reached; rather what was reproposed was an obscure, ontological breaking apart between ideal world and real world (cf. *Being and Time*, n.44 and *On the Essence of Truth*). Thus one remains within the Kantian scheme of the separation between thought and being, ideal and real. What contributed to this outcome was the radical anti-intellectualism of Heidegger and a lack of reflection on his part on the nature of knowledge. What took its place was a proposal to remain open and at the disposal of what, within the history of being, manifests itself in a clearing.[9]

This proposed elaboration includes this significant result: the doctrine of truth as conformity leads to the thesis that being-in-the-world, the historical structures, the hermeneutical understandings, cannot erase the existence of truths and of criteria of truth which are independent of time or above it. Besides different interpretations indefinitely renewable according to the different eras and cultures, the possibility in principle of assertions which are simply true is thus founded.

Notes

1   Nietzsche, *On Truth and Lie in an Extramoral Sense*, I.
2   *Riflessioni sull'intelligenza*, Milan: Massimo, 1987, p.41.
3   *I gradi del sapere*, Brescia: Morcelliana, 1974, p.117.
4   Ibid., pp.114f. On this vital issue refer to V. Possenti, *Approssimazioni all'essere*, Padua: Il Poligrafo, 1995, pp.28–34.
5   For the convenience of the reader, I have gathered together some significant propositions of the *Tractatus* on this matter:

    2.12 The image (*Bild*) is a model of reality.
    2.131 The elements of the image are representatives of the objects within the image.
    2.15 The fact that the elements of the image are in a determinate relation with each other signifies that things are in such a relation with each other.
    2.151 The form of representation (*Abbildung*) is the possibility that things are in relation to each other in the same way as the elements of the image are in relation to each other.
    2.161 Within the image and the represented (*In Bild und Abgebildetem*) something must be identical (*identisch*), so that that one can be an image of this one.
    2.19 The logical image can represent the world.
    3. The logical image of the facts is thought (*Gedanke*).
6   *Tempo ed essere*, Naples: Guida 1980, p.185.
7   *Nietzsche*, Milan: Adelphi, 1994. p.938.
8   Cf. *Being and Time*, n.44.
9   One can read some interesting exerpts from Aristotle and Hegel where, differently from what we find with Kant and Heidegger, the question of intentionality of thought and of intentional identity between thought and object are adequately treated.
    'In general, the intellect when it is in act, is its objects', *De anima*, 431 b 18s. Even on a sensible level the act of the sensible and of the sense are one and the same act (425b 26s).
    For Hegel the old metaphysics belonging to the pre-critical period had a higher concept of thought, since it held that 'things and the thinking of things ... coincided in and with each other, that thought with its immanent determinations and the true nature of things were one and the same content'. Cf. *Science of Logic*, introduction, where the Hegelian controversy about the 'thing in itself' and the purported separation between the phenomenon and the noumenon, thought and object, is relentless.

Nihilism, Ontotheology, Analogia Entis

One of the most important tasks of *Fides et Ratio* is the diagnosis of nihilism. By conferring on it a dramatic characteristic, it addresses philosophy and believing thought which could well find in nihilism the great issue on which to reflect for a revival within existence and knowledge. As we have already seen, it is tied to the ignoring or the rejection of the sense of being, followed by the oblivion of being and the loss of contact with objective truth. This diagnosis, while identifying the root problem, leaves much unexpressed. By dwelling in its conceptual space, we need to catch what is not said, beginning with the element for which the rejection of the sense of being leads to another significant core issue which could be formulated thus: the oblivion of being includes the oblivion and ultimately the refusal of the *analogia entis* and of ontotheology. This rejection is often motivated by a desire, more or less conscious, to deconstruct the concept of God perceived as an obstacle to the radical nature of the philosophical task, and to deny the identity between God and Being (*Esse*). The criticism of ontotheology and of analogy, taken for granted as a commonplace in many currents of thought, is usually developed by adopting Heidegger's philosophy as an inspiration. But there is scarce awareness of a crucial point, that is, whether a philosophy such as Heidegger's, which claims to remain within the finite and the insuperable transcendental circle of temporality, is adequate for pronouncements (be they affirmative or critical) on the infinite, on what rests outside that circle. To attack ontotheology and the *analogia entis* on those premises is like biting granite.

The Heideggerian critique is found in numerous passages. Significant are those present in the essay 'Identity and Difference', and especially those on 'the onto-theo-logic constitution of metaphysics'. They support the assumption according to which God is thought of by ontotheology as the supreme being (*summum ens*) and as *causa sui*. It is not an adequate solution to attribute this colossal equivocation to the scant historiographical information of Heidegger, which nevertheless has its role (where and when have the best accredited natural theologies thought of God who enters into philosophy as *causa sui*?). In reality two mutually untenable positions are sustained: on one side the limitation of ontotheology is individuated as that of having thought of God as an entity (*ens*) and not as being (*esse*), on the other side it is considered impossible to establish an identity between God and being (*esse*). There are notable passages in *Beiträge zur Philosophie* where God is defined as undefectible need of being (*Notschaft des Seyns*), as if He were inhabited by an obscure hunger. In this respect other passages are also important where the equation *Deus = Esse* is negated with a clarity which leaves nothing to be desired:

Being and God are not identical, and I would never try to think God's essence
through being. Some know that I come from theology and that I have kept alive
an old love for it, and that I understand something about it. Were I to write a
theology – and sometimes I feel like doing so – I would never let the term
'being' appear in it. Faith has no need of being. Once it uses it, it is no longer
faith... I believe that being can never be thought as essence and foundation for
God.[1]

In these passages two aversions are expressed: one is anti-Hellenic and the
other is anti-biblical, since in the Bible the attribution of being to God is
common. This is an intrinsic part of the idea that He is original Perfection, not
a God who creates Himself, who is hunger for being, not a God to come, very
similar to 'the last God' introduced by the *Beiträge*. In Heideggerian thought,
by denying that faith remains such when it turns to being, the risk of ending
up in an ontophobia is high. In no ontotheology has the problem of the
difference between *ens* and *esse* been thought out so profoundly as in that of
Seinsphilosophie, where the identity Deus = Esse is asserted, and hence His
infinite distance from beings (*entia*), His value as Unique and Other are
maintained. Only thinking of God as *Esse* can one perceive the difference
between being as *esse* and being as *ens*. This enormous development escaped
Heidegger, who even here was unable to avoid the oblivion of being.

These criticisms of ontotheology, as incapable of thinking of the infinite
difference between being and God, are often voiced alongside those against
analogia entis, understood as a conciliatory modality, in the sense of a
proximity of similitude between finite and infinite rather than in the sense of
an enormous difference. Those who would like to reflect a little on the issue
and arrive at some clear notion regarding the pretentious character of the
above criticism, may be helped by a reading of a sentence of the Lateranense
Council IV (1215): 'Inter creatorem et creaturam non potest tanta similitudo
notari, quin inter eos major sit dissimilitudo notanda' (Between creator and
creature it cannot be observed so much similarity, that between them greater
is the dissimilarity which can be observed) (Denz. n.432). This implies that
God's knowledge, which can be reached through the knowledge of finite
things, is indirect, within a mystery (*in aenigmate*), absolutely non-exhaustive
and incapable of grasping its essence. On these elements there is a continuity
from Augustine to Anselm, from Bonaventure to Aquinas, all the way up to
the modern believing thought which escapes the oblivion of being.

On this subject there are meaningful paragraphs, full of equilibrium and
just measure, written by Maritain in his *The Degrees of Knowledge*, regarding the knowledge of God attainable by human search. Aquinas' theology
does nothing else but follow this gain when it proclaims, 'de Deo quid sit
penitus manet ignotum'.[2] The *analogia entis*, a bridge thrown between finite
and infinite, is a non-circumscribable kind of analogy, which neither cir-
cumscribes nor exhausts its divine object. Direct knowability is the characteristic of idols: only they can be directly known.

Whenever this attack on ontotheology and the *analogia entis* is fully
carried out and understood in its potentialities, an anti-creationist principle

reveals itself. In its most radical manifestations, this expresses itself as a refusal of God the creator and of His transcendental all-encompassing causality. This implies such a drastic separation between First Cause and secondary causes, between Creator and creatures, that in a real sense there is no longer a Creator and neither is there a creature. At the bottom of the attack on ontotheology and on *analogia entis* (which can be an immediate metaphysical implication of the creationist principle) may lie an anti-divine element, a will to an absolute separation between God (who is far, stranger, perhaps hostile) and man. This dangerous element escaped Barth who, caught in a polemical argument tending to demonize the *analogia entis*, undervalued the disruptive implications of his refusal.[3] Those who, eulogizing Heidegger and Barth, consider the critique of ontotheology beyond criticism and refuse the identity Deus = Esse, also operate imprudently. Those premises seem to originate in a radical agnosticism according to which philosophy, understood as an aporetic dialectic that can be turned inside-out like a glove, does not know anything.

Now a Christian theology without creation has no right to such a name. Therefore those roads where creation and redemption are separated lead nowhere. By accepting redemption and forgetting creation, the oblivion of being, of creation and of causality come together and may be defined, together, as well each in its own right, as nihilism. In its extreme cases one can glimpse an obscure anti-divine position. Neither is it an adequate path to think of creation without rooting it in a universal all-pervading First Cause, which at every moment activates every created existent, saving it from *vertibilitas in nihilum* congenial to it, and thus activating in it the first and radical act of existence (*esse*), which dwells as a tranquil and unmovable act within the heart of the existent. The very first, the most intimate and immediate effect of all-pervading divine causality is the *esse/actus essendi*, which is proper to every being. *The Book of Wisdom*, by clearing the path to the speculative development of ontotheology and of the *analogia entis*, observes that 'From the greatness and the beauty of creatures one can know by analogy its author' (13:5). This criterion opens up the eternal road, closed to those who dwell in the shadow of nihilism, by which man may attain some knowledge of the absolute.[4]

Notes

1   'Seminare', in *Gesamtausgabe*, vol. 15, Frankfurt A.M: Klostermann, p.437. On those aspects see V. Possenti, *Approssimazioni all'essere*, Padua: Il Poligrafo, 1995, pp.99–106.

2   *Summa contra Gentes*, l. III, c.49. The employment of the *analogia entis* to attain a certain knowledge of God does not consider God as similar to creatures; rather, in a deficient way, it considers the creatures similar to God in virtue of the similarity between the effect and the cause. What God does or has done is the source of the knowledge we have of Him. Divine being is different from any other: 'Esse divinum, quod est ejus substantia, non est esse commune, sed est esse distinctum a quolibet alio esse. Unde per ipsum suum esse Deus differt a quolibet alio ente' (*De Potentia*, q.7, a.2, ad 4m).

3   According to K. Barth, the *analogia entis* must be considered an invention of the Anti-
    Christ. It is the main reason why one should not become a Catholic (see the preface to
    the first volume of *Kirchliche Dogmatik*). It is quite clear that the condemnation of the
    analogia entis implies that of natural theology and the employment of the *analogia fidei*
    only. The two analogies cannot be employed together synergetically since they are in
    Barth mutually exclusive. A recourse to analogy (be it only that of faith) is however
    indispensable, even for him. Without it one would fall into equivocation and univocation:
    the first would render impossible any knowledge of God, the other either lowers God or
    divinizes man. Having accepted only the *analogia fidei*, the analogy between God and
    the world is, according to Barth, something that is totally independent from philosophy
    and totally dependent on Revelation. According to H. Chavannes, who has accurately
    studied the issue (*L'analogie entre Dieu et le monde*, Paris: Cerf, 1969), Barth has run
    into an equivocation, confusing the peculiar conception of the *analogia entis* as under-
    stood by E. Przywara with the Catholic and Thomistic kind of which he seemed to have
    a rather inadequate knowledge. The author suggests that we consider the limits inherent
    to the Barthian ontology and his doctrine of knowledge, with its post-Kantian style and
    idealistic streaks, where the object that is known is changed in its being by the knowing
    subject. There is also present in Barth the premise that philosophy can reach only what
    is abstract and neuter, never existence. Probably what he had before him as a paradigm
    for philosophizing was that of modern rationalism, enmeshed in the impossibility of
    reaching existence.

4   Within 'negative thought' nurtured by the criticism of the *analogia entis* and of
    ontotheology, there is a refusal of the natural knowability of things as mediated by first
    principles (the principles of non-contradiction, of causality, of finality). Their abandon-
    ment, together with the denial of their transcendental validity, is nothing else but a
    corollary of the oblivion of being since those first principles can be formulated and are
    valid only in relationship to being.

Index of Names